Series / Number 07-059

# META-ANALYSIS
## Quantitative Methods for Research Synthesis

**FREDRIC M. WOLF**
*University of Michigan*

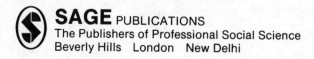

**SAGE** PUBLICATIONS
The Publishers of Professional Social Science
Beverly Hills   London   New Delhi

*To Leora*

*For information address:*

SAGE Publications, Inc.
275 South Beverly Drive
Beverly Hills, California 90212

SAGE Publications India Pvt. Ltd.
M-32 Market
Greater Kailash I
New Delhi 110 048 India

SAGE Publications Ltd
28 Banner Street
London EC1Y 8QE
England

International Standard Book Number 0-8039-2756-8

Library of Congress Catalog Card No. 85-052372

FIRST PRINTING

When citing a university paper, please use the proper form. Remember to cite the correct
Sage University Paper series title and include the paper number. One of the following
formats can be adapted (depending on the style manual used):

(1) IVERSEN, GUDMUND R. and NORPOTH, HELMUT (1976) "Analysis of
Variance." Sage University Paper series on Quantitative Applications in the Social
Sciences, 07-001. Beverly Hills: Sage Pubns.

*OR*

(2) Iversen, Gudmund R. and Norpoth, Helmut. 1976. *Analysis of Variance*. Sage
University Paper series on Quantitative Applications in the Social Sciences, series no.
07-001. Beverly Hills: Sage Pubns.

# CONTENTS

## Series Editor's Introduction

Single experiments or studies in the social and behavioral sciences rarely provide definitive answers to research questions. Rather, if science in the social and behavioral domains is to progress, it must be through the discovery of underlying trends and principles developed from the accumulation and refinement of a large body of studies. Thus literature reviews of empirical research play an important role in summarizing and clarifying the state of science at a given point in time. Yet traditional, narrative reviews suffer from their dependence on the subjective judgments, preferences, and biases of the reviewers and from the disparate definitions, variables, procedures, and samples of the original investigators.

*Meta-Analysis: Quantitative Methods for Research Synthesis,* by Fredric Wolf, is designed as an introduction to an alternative approach to narrative literature reviews. Building on both previously developed and new methods, meta-analysis itself has proliferated during the last 10 years. Meta-analysis is the application of statistical procedures to collections of empirical findings from individual studies for the purpose of integrating, synthesizing, and making sense of them. The method can be appropriately applied in numerous areas within all the social, behavioral, and biomedical sciences.

Wolf begins Chapter 1 with a brief overview of the method along with a discussion of the advantages and criticisms of meta-analysis. Chapter 2 presents three of the more common statistical tests for combining the results of independent tests of the same hypothesis. Chapter 3 deals with measures of effect size for studies of both group differences and correlational relationships. The chapter concludes with discussions of how to select a common metric in order to aggregate diverse statistics across studies and of methods for examining possible interactions or mediating effects.

Chapter 4 discusses how to examine issues that may bias the results of a meta-analysis. Among the topics covered are the so-called file drawer problem, weighting and unbiased estimates, tests of homogeneity, nonindependent results, validity, and reliability. Chapter 5 includes a brief overview of nonparametric analysis and adds substantially to the balance and comprehensiveness of the volume. Chapter 6 concludes the text with a review of the limitations and strengths of meta-analysis. It also contains practical guidelines that provide an excellent outline of the steps necessary to conduct an appropriate meta-analysis.

This volume is exceptionally readable and is suitable for anyone with a background in elementary statistics. Its clear presentation derives in part from the fact that Wolf makes good use of examples and illustrations. Also helpful is that he tells us not only how to interpret results but also how to make many of the appropriate calculations. Overall, Wolf's *Meta-Analysis* makes an excellent addition to Sage's *Quantitative Applications in the Social Sciences* series.

*—Richard G. Niemi*
Series Co-Editor

## Acknowledgments

I am grateful to James A. Kulik, Richard G. Niemi, Michael Q. Patton, William H. Yeaton, and the anonymous referees for their helpful comments and suggestions, and to Richard G. Cornell and Robert Rosenthal for their helpful discussions of some of the statistical procedures.

## Acknowledgments

# META-ANALYSIS:

# Quantitative Methods for Research Synthesis

**FREDRIC M. WOLF**
*University of Michigan*

## 1. META-ANALYSIS AND SYNTHESIZING RESEARCH

**Research activity in the** social and behavioral sciences has been observed to be "sadly dilapidated" and facing a "crisis" situation (Glass, 1977; Glass, McGaw, and Smith, 1981; Hunter, Schmidt, and Jackson, 1982; Jackson, 1980; Rosenthal, 1984). The biological, physical, and natural sciences often allow research problems to be clearly defined and examined by commonly accepted and standardized techniques and methods. This often leads to scientific understanding and progress in which tidy, straightforward answers to problems studied under experimental conditions are obtained in a logical, sequential fashion, building on each other. This is *not* the case in the social and behavioral sciences where human behavior is often more difficult and complex to explain, where research environments are more difficult to control, common definitions are not always available nor accepted, and where methods, techniques, and sampling characteristics vary from study to study. Rarely do "single experiments or studies provide sufficiently definitive answers upon which to base policy" (Hedges and Olkin, 1982). This situation is all the more difficult because of the proliferation of studies in the social and behavioral sciences that address common research questions. For example, hundreds of studies have examined the psychology of sex differences, the efficacy of psychotherapy, and the relationship of socioeconomic status to achievement or of individual characteristics and contextual variables to voting preferences and patterns. These studies not only use disparate definitions, variables, procedures, methods, samples, and so on, but their conclusions are often at odds with each other.

The effect of this situation leads to an "enormous waste of scholarly effort in the social sciences" (Kulik, 1983), conflicting results which can lead to no "acceptable" answers to guide policy for the problems posed but instead yield unending calls for further research, and the danger that funding agencies may increasingly view social and behavioral research as muddled, unproductive, and unscientific. Furthermore, literature reviews of empirical studies often go professionally unrewarded and are notorious for depending on the subjective judgments, preferences, and biases of the reviewers; conflicting interpretations of the evidence are not uncommon, while even consistent interpretations by independent reviewers may be built on similar biases and misreadings of the literature (Light and Smith, 1971; Glass, 1977; Pillemer and Light, 1980; Jackson, 1980).

## Advantages of Meta-Analytic Literature Reviews

If we view science as the accumulation and refinement of information and knowledge (Hunter et al., 1982; Pillemer and Light, 1980), it then becomes critical to establish guidelines for reliable and valid reviews, integrations, and syntheses of studies examining similar research questions (Cooper, 1982; Jackson, 1980). Procedures employed in meta-analysis permit quantitative reviews and syntheses of the research literature that address these issues.

Potential problems with traditional literature reviews that are addressed in meta-analysis include (1) selective inclusion of studies, often based on the reviewer's own impressionistic view of the quality of the study, (2) differential subjective weighting of studies in the interpretation of a set of findings, (3) misleading interpretations of study findings, (4) failure to examine characteristics of the studies as potential explanations for disparate or consistent results across studies, and (5) failure to examine moderating variables in the relationship under examination.

"What is needed are methods that will integrate results from existing studies to reveal patterns of relatively invariant underlying relations and causalities, the establishment of which will constitute general principles and cumulative knowledge" (Hunter et al., 1982: 26). The "fundamental problem," as Glass et al. (1981) refer to it, is the inability of the human mind to address this task reliably and validly given the enormous amount of data that must be gathered, processed, assimilated, and synthesized in many disciplines. It is ironic that the traditional review of scientific data has typically been done in an unscientific, impressionistic fashion. It has been argued that the same scientific rigor be applied to research literature reviews as to individual empirically designed studies to address the research question at hand. "Contemporary research reviewing should be more technical and statistical than it is narrative. . . . The findings of multiple studies should be regarded as a complex data set, no more comprehensible without statistical analysis than would hundreds of data points in one study" (Glass et al., 1981: 12).

The statistical methods proposed by Glass and others to accomplish this task are generally well known but applied in a difficult context. Each data point used for analysis is obtained from an individual study rather than from an individual subject, as is typically done in a traditional research study.

Glass (1976: 3) distinguished among the primary, secondary and meta-analysis of research:

> *Primary analysis* is the original analysis of data in a research study. . . . *Secondary analysis* is the re-analysis of data for the purpose of answering the original research question with better statistical techniques, or answering new questions with old data. . . . *Meta-analysis* refers to the analysis of analyses . . . the statistical analysis of a large collection of analysis results from individual studies for the purpose of integrating the findings. It connotes a rigorous alternative to the casual, narrative discussions of research studies which typify our attempts to make sense of the rapidly expanding research literature.

## Illustrative Examples of Meta-Analysis

The following examples of published meta-analyses illustrate the utility of this approach for reviews of research literature. Mazzuca (1982) initially examined over 300 articles addressing the research question of whether patient education in chronic disease has therapeutic value. Those 30 studies using true experimental designs were then selected for meta-analysis. Among the conclusions drawn from this analysis were that patient education significantly improved regimen compliance, therapeutic progress, and health outcomes for those individuals who received it (in comparison with control subjects). However, the impact of patient education was greatest for compliance and least for health outcomes, and consistently stronger for behaviorally, in contrast to didactly, oriented interventions. For example, there was a median improvement of 0.74 standard deviation units in therapeutic progress for subjects receiving behaviorally oriented patient education and only 0.18 standard deviation units of improvement for didactic instruction. Thus the average patient who receives education with a behavioral emphasis would be expected to demonstrate a physiological response to therapy better than that of 78 percent of the control patients.

In another meta-analysis, Willson and Putnam (1982) studied the effects of pretest sensitization in experimental design by examining the contribution of pretests to variables assessing human educational or psychological performance. More than 160 separate statistical effects were initially examined from 32 independent studies; 30 effects from the nonrandomized studies were eliminated from further examination as a result of their mean effect size differing significantly from the average randomized study effect size. Willson and Putnam concluded that the nonrandomized study effects exhibited systematic but unknown bias and therefore should be excluded from further analysis. Among the conclusions drawn from the remaining 134 study effects was that, on the average, pretests had a general elevating effect on posttests of 0.22 standard deviation units. The elevating effect was greater for cognitive and personality outcomes and less for attitude outcomes. Duration of time between pre- and posttesting was related to the magnitude of the effect sizes, with smaller effects associated with durations less than one day or more than one month.

These findings may be compared to an earlier traditional literature review that summarized the significance or nonsignificance of the individual study results and that impressionistically concluded that long-term cognitive effects are small or nil, although there may be short-term effects (Welch and Walberg, 1970). Welch and Walberg suggested that the effect is greater for attitude rather than for cognitive tests, in contrast to the empirically derived results of Willson and Putnam's meta-analysis. As a practical matter, Willson and Putnam's results suggest that researchers need to include pretest as a design variable when it is present and to estimate its effect, particularly in situations above where its effects have been shown to be strongest.

In a relatively early example of synthesizing the literature involving 140 case studies on technological innovations in local services, Yin, Bingham, and Heald (1976) found that the methodological quality of the case studies reported was not related to whether the innovation had been incorporated into a routine part of agency operations, nor to whether there were measurable gains in services as a result of the innovation. However, higher (in contrast to lower) quality case studies were significantly more likely to involve client participation and to focus on hardware innovations, public works, and transportation services.

While Glass and his colleagues reawakened the contemporary social science research community to the importance of systematically evaluating and synthesizing the results of independent tests of the same hypothesis, interest in this question can be traced back at least to the work of L.H.C. Tippett (1931), R. A. Fisher (1932), Karl Pearson (1933), and W. G. Cochran (1937). This early work stemmed largely from the desire to combine evidence from different agricultural studies and took two different, yet complementary, approaches. One approach focuses on testing the statistical significance of the combined results across primary research studies, while the other approach focuses on the estimation of the magnitude of the experimental effect (treatment) across these studies. The former have become known as combined tests and range from various simple counting procedures involving either significance levels (probabilities or their logarithmic transformations) or raw or weighted test statistics such as $t$'s or $z$'s. The most common combined test methods are presented in Chapter 2 of this monograph. The other approach refers to measures of effect size and are based on developing standardized, scale-invariant indexes of the magnitude of effects that are independent of the various scales of measurement used in the original studies (see Chapter 3).

Early attempts at the quantification of research domains focused on what have become known as "vote-counting" methods (Light and Smith, 1971), in which reviewers sort the results of each study into positive significant, nonsignificant, and negative significant categories. Conclusions are then based on the resulting tallies. The vote-counting approach is no longer recommended because of the poor statistical properties associated with its use. For example, Hedges and Olkin (1980) have found the power of this procedure to be low and actually decrease as the number of studies reviewed increases, and to have a high probability of a type II error (failing to conclude that there is a positive effect when in fact there is). Because of these limitations and the decreasing use of this procedure, this method will not be discussed further in the present presentation; this method has largely been superseded by the use of combined tests. Interested readers are referred to Hedges and Olkin (1980) for a more detailed discussion and critique of vote-counting methods.

## Criticisms of Meta-Analysis

As might be anticipated with the introduction of any new approach such as meta-analysis, this approach has not been free from criticism, nor is it a panacea for resolving all the problems associated with building reliable and valid scientific knowledge and theory. While this book will not address these criticisms in depth, it is important for informed researchers to be alerted to these potential problems and issues when reading published meta-analyses or designing their own meta-analyses. Glass et al. (1981) have grouped these criticisms into four categories:

(1) Logical conclusions cannot be drawn by comparing and aggregating studies that include different measuring techniques, definitions of variables (e.g., treatments, outcomes), and subjects because they are too dissimilar.

(2) Results of meta-analyses are uninterpretable because results from "poorly" designed studies are included along with results from "good" studies.

(3) Published research is biased in favor of significant findings because nonsignificant findings are rarely published; this in turn leads to biased meta-analysis results.

(4) Multiple results from the same study are often used which may bias or invalidate the meta-analysis and make the results appear more reliable than they really are, because these results are not independent.

The first criticism has been referred to as the "apples and oranges problem," in that it is argued that diversity makes comparisons inappropriate. For example, in one of the first meta-analyses, Smith and Glass (1977) synthesized the results of approximately 400 evaluations of the efficacy of psychotherapy and found (1) that the average therapy client is better off than 75 percent of untreated individuals and (2) virtually no difference between behavioral and nonbehavioral therapies. Presby (1978: 514) criticized Smith and Glass for ignoring "important differences among the nonbehavioral therapies, for example, the superior effects of rational-emotive therapy (RET) as compared to the others in that class. These differences are cancelled in the use of very broad categories, i.e., mixing 'apples and oranges,' which leads to the erroneous conclusion that research results indicate negligible differences among outcomes of different therapies." Similarly, Slavin (1983) took exception with the definitions of cooperation, competition, and achievement used in a meta-analysis conducted by Johnson et al. (1981). These definitions and criteria clearly affect the type of study to be included in the research synthesis, which may affect the results that follow. This issue may be dealt with empirically by coding the characteristics for each study and statistically testing whether these differences are related to the meta-analytic results. Even the most prevalent problem of differing operational definitions and measurement procedures for dependent variables may be examined empirically. One method for accomplishing this is discussed in Chapter 3 under the discussion of mediating effects.

The second criticism can also be handled empirically within meta-analyses by coding the quality of the design employed in each study and examining whether the results differ for poorly and well designed studies. A review of meta-analyses that have been done thus far suggests that the magnitude of the effect is unrelated to the worthiness of the design in some research domains but not in others. Even though no significant differences in effect size between poorly and well designed studies may be found in a meta-analysis, there may be considerably more effect size variation among "poorly" designed than well-designed studies (i.e., a significant difference in variance).

The third criticism, relating to the nontypicality and bias in favor of significant results in published research studies, can be addressed in several ways. One approach is to review results in books, dissertations, unpublished papers presented at professional meetings, and the like and compare them to the results for published articles. Another approach is to estimate the number of additional studies with nonsignificant results that would be necessary to reverse a conclusion drawn from the meta-analysis, thus providing some estimate of the robustness and validity of the findings. This approach is described and illustrated in detail in Chapter 4 in the section describing the fail-safe N and file drawer problem.

The fourth criticism concerns the number of results from the same experimental study that should be used. Some meta-analysts (e.g., Kulik, 1983; Mazzuca, 1982) choose to perform separate analyses for each different outcome (criterion or dependent variable), while others, including Glass, choose to lump them into the same analysis. Alternatively, some reviewers choose to limit themselves to a fixed number of results, perhaps two, from each study (e.g., Gilbert, McPeek, and Mosteller, 1977), while others take the average of all results from the same study. Again, this is an empirically answerable issue that may influence the obtained results and is discussed in more detail in Chapter 4.

Other criticisms of meta-analysis include the assertion that interaction effects are ignored at the expense of main effects (Cook and Leviton, 1980; Slavin, 1983). Again, this can be addressed by examining the potential mediating effects of substantive and methodological characteristics of studies (see Chapter 3). Cooper and Arkin (1981) suggest the possibility of focusing future meta-analyses on particular effects for clearly articulated interaction hypotheses.

What may be the most important caveat is that "meta-analysis can have mischievous consequences because of its apparent 'objectivity,' 'precision,' and 'scientism.' To naive readers these lend social credibility that may be built on procedural invalidity" (Cook and Leviton, 1980: 455). However, it has been pointed out (Cooper and Arkin, 1981) that this statement is true for any innovative methodology and that this problem resides within the particular use and user rather than in the method per se. The discussion in Chapter 4 of ways to reduce bias and the guidelines for practice in Chapter 6 should be useful in helping to enhance the "objectivity" of conducting a meta-analysis.

It should be noted that there are great differences in the quality of meta-analyses regarding issues of validity and reliability. These issues are discussed in Chapter 4. Slavin (1983: 14) maintains: "What traditional reviews usually do that meta-analyses do not is discuss the studies being reviewed, looking for patterns and inconsistencies, and placing more weight on studies that use strong designs than on numbers of studies falling on one or the other side of an issue." He advocates the use of meta-analysis to "enhance rather than replace an intelligent discussion of the critical issues." It is essential that sufficient information on the coding procedures for studies in a meta-analysis be presented so that the methodological rigor of the particular application can be determined. Excellent detailed summaries of how to approach the location, retrieval, and coding of studies are presented in Glass et al. (1981) and Hunter et al. (1982) and are not included here.

It has also been suggested that nonparametric rather than parametric statistics are more appropriate in the quantitative analyses of results from independent studies because distributions of effect sizes are often highly skewed (Slavin, 1983; Kraemer and Andrews, 1982). Nonparametric methods have been incorporated into several meta-analyses (e.g., Hyde, 1981; Kraemer and Andrews, 1982; Mazzuca, 1982), and several of these approaches are described in Chapter 5.

## Nonreview Applications of Procedures Used in Meta-Analysis

It should be pointed out that several of the procedures employed in meta-analytic reviews of research may be used appropriately in nonliterature review situations. Effect size measures are appropriate and helpful in primary research studies to examine the strength of the relationship or treatment and its practical importance and meaningfulness, and to complement traditional statistical tests. Aggregating statistics and effect sizes from successive implementations of a training or educational program are appropriate in program evaluation to provide more stable, reliable, and valid estimates of the efficacy of the program. An example of the practical insight provided by this approach into the repeated implementation of a training program over time is provided by Wolf et al. (1984). This type of aggregation has several pleasing properties, including the use of similar procedures, definitions, and measurement tools across the different samples of subjects, which enhances the validity of the findings, as well as mitigating the "apples and oranges" and several other criticisms of meta-analysis research reviews.

Additionally, combined tests and measures of effect size can be applied to large databases collected at multiple occasions or from different samples. For example, these procedures could be applied to the 1972-1985 cumulative data file for the General Social Survey conducted by the National Opinion Research Center. Similarly, the U.S. Bureau of the Census makes available demographic, economic, and social data for 203 countries in its International Data Base, while the National Center for Health Statistics collects a wide range of health data at various points in time and in different geographic areas of the country.

The remaining chapters summarize the most widely used combined tests (Chapter 2); effect size measures for both group differences and correlational relationships, with attention to selecting common metrics and examining potential mediating effects (Chapter 3); procedures for examining and reducing bias and enhancing the validity and reliability of meta-analysis results (Chapter 4); nonparametric approaches to meta-analysis (Chapter 5); and some of the limitations and strengths of meta-analysis and guidelines for practice (Chapter 6). Finally, the bibliography contains a comprehensive listing of both methodological references and illustrations of published meta-analyses. The interested reader is referred to Hedges and Olkin (1985) and Rosenthal (1984), as well as Glass et al. (1981) and Hunter et al. (1982) for a discussion of some of the more technical methodological issues concerning meta-analysis and research synthesis. Light and Pillemer (1982, 1984) provide thoughtful discussions of using both quantitative and qualitative approaches in combination when reviewing a research domain.

## 2. COMBINED TESTS

Since R. A. Fisher (1932) and Karl Pearson (1933) independently addressed the issue of statistically summarizing the results of independent tests of the same hypothesis, interest in these types of procedures has continued. More recently this process has been called meta-analysis, for "statistical analysis of a large collection of analysis results from individual studies for the purpose of integrating the findings" (Glass, 1976: 3). The methods reviewed here are applied to the analysis of results of the same hypothesis from different studies for the purpose of obtaining a summary overall test of the hypothesis.

Statistical methods available for combining the results of independent studies range from various counting procedures to a variety of summation procedures involving either significance levels (probabilities or their logarithmic transformations) or raw or weighted test statistics such as t-test and z-test statistics. These procedures have become known as "combined tests" and have been illustrated by Rosenthal (1978a) and Winer (1971), among others. While a variety of tests for combining the results of independent tests of the same hypothesis have been put forward (see Birnbaum, 1954; Rosenthal, 1978a; van Zwet and Oosterhoff, 1967, for reviews of these tests), only the procedures presented by Fisher (1932, 1948), Winer (1971), and Stouffer et al. (1949; Mosteller and Bush, 1954) will be discussed here.

### Fisher Combined Test

In addressing the question of combining the results of a number of independent tests which have all been planned to test a common hypothesis, Fisher described a method based on the product of probabilities from different trials. If the natural logarithms of these probabilities are calculated, multiplied by minus two (–2), and then summed, a $\chi^2$ statistic with degrees of freedom equal to two times the number of tests combined (2n) is obtained. The logarithmic transformation permits a summative rather than a multiplicative function, thereby simplifying calculations. This may be expressed as

$$\chi^2 = -2 \; \Sigma \; \log_e p \qquad\qquad [1]$$

The $\chi^2$ statistic obtained in equation 1 has a sampling distribution which is approximated by the chi square distribution with degrees of freedom equal to 2n where n = number of tests combined and p = one-tailed probability associated with each test.

This procedure has been shown to be more asymptotically optimal than some other combining methods (e.g., Koziol and Perlman, 1978; Littell and Folks, 1973), although it suffers from several limitations (Rosenthal, 1978a). Mosteller and Bush (1954) note that it can yield results inconsistent with a simple sign test in situations where the majority of a number of studies showed results in one direction with *p* values close to .50 (i.e., chance). In this situation the sign test could easily reject the overall null hypothesis, while the Fisher procedure would not. The Fisher procedure would thus yield more conservative results in this situation, a result not terribly disturbing given the recent recommendations of reporting the effect size as well as the overall probability level when using combined tests (McGaw and Glass, 1980; Rosenthal, 1978a). That is, while the sign test would be significant in this instance, the effect size would likely be small and thus more appropriately tested with the Fisher method, which would result in nonsignificance.

A more serious disadvantage of the Fisher procedure is its support for the significance of either outcome when two studies of equally and strongly significant results in opposite directions are obtained. For example, Adcock (1960) describes a situation where $p < .001$ favoring the experimental group and $p < .001$ favoring the control group combine for a $p < .01$ using the Fisher procedure. In this instance the Fisher combined test supports the significance of either outcome. Despite these limitations, this procedure remains one of the best known and applied.

## Winer Combined Test

Winer (1971) presents a procedure for combining independent tests that comes directly from the sampling distribution of independent t-statistics in which the t-statistics associated with each test are summed and divided by the square root of the sum of the degrees of freedom (df) associated with each t after each df has been divided by df –2. This may be expressed in the form

$$Z_c = \frac{\Sigma t}{\sqrt{\Sigma [df/(df-2)]}} \qquad [2]$$

This procedure is based on $df/(df - 2)$ being the variance of a t distribution, which is approximately normally distributed (N [0, 1]) when $df \geq 10$. Thus this procedure is not appropriate for tests based on very small samples (less than 10). In practice, however, it is not common for tests of significance to be applied to such small samples, thereby minimizing the effect of this disadvantage.

**Stouffer Combined Test**

A third approach originally attributed to Stouffer et al. (1949) is more fully described by Mosteller and Bush (1954) and Rosenthal (1978a). It is similar to the Winer procedure of summing t's, with the exception that *p* values are converted to z's instead of to t's, and then summed. The denominator then simplifies to the square root of the number of tests combined, and the complete expression takes the form

$$Z_c = \frac{\Sigma z}{\sqrt{N}} \qquad [3]$$

where N = the number of tests combined. This procedure is based on the sum of normal deviates being itself a normal deviate, with the variance equal to the number of observations summed.

The Stouffer procedure offers several advantages. The calculations are more straightforward than either the Fisher procedure, which necessitates logarithmic transformations, or the Winer procedure, which makes an adjustment for degrees of freedom. In addition, results of the z procedure, while slightly more powerful, are virtually identical to results of the t procedure (Wolf and Spies, 1981). This is particularly true when the statistics summed are derived from large samples, as $df/df - 2$ approaches unity as the sample size increases.

## TABLE 1
### Hypothetical Results of Four Studies Examining
### the Effects of Exercise on Self-Esteem

| Study | Control Group | | Experimental Group | | Within sd | t |
|---|---|---|---|---|---|---|
| | n | $\overline{X}$ | n | $\overline{X}$ | | |
| A | 41 | 11 | 41 | 17 | 16 | 2.72** |
| B | 29 | 225 | 33 | 175 | 100 | −1.95 |
| C | 104 | 9 | 98 | 12 | 7 | 2.03* |
| D | 11 | 23 | 11 | 31 | 12 | 1.56 |

*p < .05, two-tailed test; **p < .01, two-tailed test.

### Illustrative Numerical Examples

Suppose we wanted to review previous studies that tested the hypothesis that exercising can enhance an individual's self-concept or self-esteem and our literature review located only four studies addressing this research question. Table 1 presents the results of these four fictitional studies. Studies A and C used the Coopersmith Self-Esteem Inventory to measure self-concept, while study A used the Tennessee Self-Concept Scale and Study D used the Rosenberg Self-Esteem Scale.

The results of these independent studies indicated significantly greater self-esteem on the average for the intervention subjects versus the control subjects in studies A ($p < .001$) and C ($p < .05$) but not in studies B and D. In fact, self-esteem was higher (nonsignificantly) for the control group than the experimental group in study B. Disparate results of this nature are not uncommon in the social and behavioral sciences, and the question remains, Can exercise improve self-esteem? In a traditional review of literature, impressionistic judgments would be made based on the reviewer's reading and understanding of each of the studies. Some studies may be considered more worthy than others, and thus some may be relied on more or less heavily in drawing conclusions. Using a combined test would allow for a statistical generalization to be made with respect to the combined evidence from all four of these studies.

The results in Table 1 have been summarized in Table 2 to facilitate the calculations of our combined tests. It should be noted that the sign preceeding t or z indicates the direction of the results, with a minus sign (−) indicating that the result was inconsistent with the majority of the

TABLE 2
Results of Four Independent Studies
Used for Calculating Combined Tests

| Study | $t$ | $df$ | one-tailed $p$ | $Z$ | $-2 \log_e p$ |
|-------|------|-----|------|-------|-------|
| A | 2.72 | 80 | .004 | 2.65 | 11.04 |
| B | -1.95 | 60 | .97 | -1.88 | 0.06 |
| C | 2.03 | 200 | .024 | 1.98 | 7.46 |
| D | 1.56 | 20 | .06 | 1.52 | 5.63 |

results. Applying formula 1 for the Fisher procedure to the results of our four studies, we obtain

$$\chi^2 = 11.04 + 0.06 + 7.46 + 5.63 = 24.19 \qquad [4]$$

Because there are four independent tests of this hypothesis, one for each study, there are 2n or (2)(4) = 8 degrees of freedom. $\chi^2 = 24.19$ is thus associated with $p < .01$.

Similarly, when applying formula 2 for the Winer procedure to the same data, the following result is obtained:

$$Z_c = \frac{2.72 - 1.95 + 2.03 + 1.56}{\sqrt{(80/78) + (60/58) + (200/198) + (20/18)}} \qquad [5]$$

$$= \frac{4.29}{\sqrt{4.18}} = \frac{4.29}{2.04} = 2.10$$

The probability of obtaining this value of $Z_c$ or one larger is $p \,(\geq 2.10) <$ .018, one-tailed. One-tailed hypothesis tests are always used because of the directional nature of the hypothesis resulting from already knowing the direction of the majority of the results from the individual studies combined in the analysis. Rosenthal (1980a) discusses this issue at greater length.

Analogous results are obtained in equation 6 when formula 3 for the Stouffer procedure is applied to the data. In this approach, however, the one-tailed $p$ values are converted to their analogous $Z$-statistics and then summed and divided by the square root of the number of tests summed. In order to obtain a reasonably exact one-tailed $p$ level, it may be necessary to use extended tables of the t distribution. These are provided by Federighi (1959) and reprinted in Rosenthal and Rosnow (1984).

$$Z_c = \frac{2.65 - 1.88 + 1.98 + 1.52}{\sqrt{4}} = \frac{4.27}{\sqrt{4}} = 2.13 \qquad [6]$$

The probability of obtaining this value $Z_c$ or larger is $p(Z \geq 2.13) < .017$, one-tailed.

Regardless which of these combined tests is used, the combined evidence from these four studies indicates that the null hypothesis of no significant effect common to each of the studies should be rejected if the scope of the inference is with respect to the combined populations. Interestingly, exercise appears to positively effect self-esteem even when results for two of these four studies are nonsignificant when examined independently. Reasons for this are discussed in the chapters on effect size and examining and reducing bias.

## Selecting a Combined Test

Practically speaking, the results of the various combined tests are typically consistent with each other. The various strengths and limitations of each have been summarized briefly. Ease of calculation may be a consideration. If the results of all the independent studies are reported as t's, then it is relatively straightforward to use the Winer procedure. If independent studies report different statistics, then transforming them to their appropriate one-tailed $p$ values is necessary for combining the results. The Fisher procedure has the advantage of being the most asymptotically efficient of the combined tests (Koziol and Perlman, 1978; Littell and Folks, 1973), but this can be weighed against the relatively straightforward calculations for the Stouffer procedure. As a practical matter, the difference in results among these procedures is slight.

## 3. MEASURES OF EFFECT SIZE

Statistical tests such as the combined procedures previously described provide a summary index of the statistical significance of the results pertaining to a hypothesis. Because statistical tests do not, however, provide any insight into the strength of the relationship or effect of interest, it is desirable to accompany combined tests with indexes of effect size.

Glass's exposition and application of meta-analysis relies heavily on the use of measures of effect size that have been eloquently summarized by Cohen (1977: 9-10):

> Without intending any necessary implication of causality, it is convenient to use the phrase "effect size" to mean "the *degree* to which the phenomenon is present in the population," or "the degree to which the null hypothesis is false." Whatever the manner of representation of a phenomenon in a particular research in the present treatment, the null hypothesis always means that the effect size is zero.

McGaw and Glass (1980) and Glass et al. (1981) provide helpful guidelines for converting various summary statistics into a common metric, usually in the form of the Pearson Product Moment Correlation. Cohen (1965, 1977) provides measures of effect size for many common statistical tests. The effect size measures for t-tests between two group means such as between experimental and control group or pretest and posttest group comparisons are illustrated here. The reader is referred to the above references for measures of effect size appropriate for statistical tests other than those that are appropriate for (1) differences between two groups as assessed by Student's t-test and (2) the degree of association between two variables as measured by the Pearson Product Moment Correlation coefficient *r*.

## Group Differences

The goal is to obtain a

> pure number, one free of our original measurement unit with which to index what can be alternatively called the degree of departure from the null hypothesis of the alternative hypothesis, or the ES (effect size) we wish to detect. This is accomplished by standardizing the raw effect size as expressed in the measurement unit of the dependent variable by dividing it by the (common) standard deviation of the measures in their respective populations, the latter also in the original measurement unit [Cohen, 1977: 20].

This may be accomplished in the form

$$d = \frac{|M_1 - M_2|}{\sigma} \qquad [7]$$

where d = the ES index for t-tests of means in standard unit, $M_1$ and $M_2$ = population means in original measurement units, and $\sigma$ = the standard deviation of either population (as homogeneity of variance is assumed). In actual practice, the sample means and standard deviation are used as approximations of their analogous population values, and equation 7 becomes

$$d = \frac{|\bar{x}_1 - \bar{x}_2|}{Sd} \qquad [8]$$

Thus the absolute value of the difference between the two group means is divided by the standard deviation to obtain the standardized, scale-invariant estimate of the size of the effect. The standard deviation is typically either the control group or pretest standard deviation, as it is assumed that the two groups' variances are equal and that these are the groups for which change is desired. Alternatively, the within (pooled) population standard deviation can be used and is preferred by some researchers.

**Illustrative Numerical Example**

Returning to our example testing the research hypothesis that exercise can improve self-concept, the results of our four independent studies in Table 1 are summarized again in Table 3. The effect size (ES) is calculated separately for each of our four studies. If equation 8 is applied to the results of study A, for example, we obtain

$$d = \frac{|11 - 17|}{10} = \frac{6}{10} = 0.60 \qquad [9]$$

The value for d is calculated in a similar fashion for the other studies. The absolute value of d (the standardized difference between the two means) is obtained and then assigned a positive (+) or negative (–) value.

**TABLE 3**
**Results and Effect Sizes for Four Independent Studies**

| Study | Group Mean Control | Group Mean Experimental | Within Sd | d | $U_3$ (%) |
|-------|---------|--------------|-----------|------|---------|
| A | 11 | 17 | 10 | 0.60 | 72.6 |
| B | 225 | 175 | 100 | −0.50 | 30.9 |
| C | 9 | 12 | 7 | 0.43 | 66.6 |
| D | 23 | 31 | 12 | 0.75 | 77.3 |
| Average | | | | 0.32 | 62.5 |

Positive values are assigned to values of d associated with results favoring the experimental (or posttest) group, while negative values are assigned to values of d associated with results favoring the control (or pretest) group. In our example, the effect sizes (d) for studies A, C, and D are assigned positive values, while the effect size for study B is assigned a negative value. Once we calculate the effect size d for each of our independent studies, we use the average of these effect sizes as calculated using formula 10 to represent the estimate of effect size across all four studies.

$$d_{average} = \frac{\Sigma d}{n} \qquad [10]$$

where d = the effect size for each independent study and n = the number of studies. Thus, for our example in Table 3, we find

$$d_{average} = \frac{0.60 - .50 + 0.43 + 0.75}{4} = 0.32 \qquad [11]$$

Based on our findings for $d_{average}$, we can say that exercise should improve self-concept by approximately 0.32 standard deviation units. This would be our best estimate regardless of how we measured self-concept, as it will be remembered that we said we used three different outcome measures as dependent variables in our four studies: the Coopersmith measure in studies A and C, the Tennessee in study B, and the Rosenberg in study C. These three measures all vary in both the number and format of the items they contain.

## Interpreting Effect Sizes for Studies of Group Differences

Once an effect size has been calculated, it is desirable and important to interpret what it means. One method of doing this is to construct a 95 or 99 percent confidence interval around the average effect size to examine whether it encompasses zero. It is customary to report the standard deviation associated with the average effect size across studies to provide some index of the variability associated with it. In our example, $0.56\,Sd_x$ is the standard deviation associated with $d_{average}$ of $0.32\,Sd_x$. It is then possible to construct confidence intervals around the average effect size, should we desire to do so. The 95 percent confidence interval for our average effect size of 0.32 in our example actually spans zero (-0.23, +0.87). It would be desirable for the average effect size *not* to encompass zero in order for us to be more certain that there is a significant effect across these studies.

Another approach is to look to the particular professional field in which the research was conducted. For example, Haase et al. (1982) calculated the distribution of effect sizes for each univariate inferential statistic reported in the *Journal of Counseling Psychology* for the years 1970-1979. They suggested that the median effect for this distribution represents one reasonable standard for comparison against which the magnitude of experimental effects in counseling psychology could be evaluated. Wolf et al. (1984) used this approach to help interpret the effects of a communication skills training program.

More often, however, no such distribution of effects in a given field is available, and often there is no standard against which to evaluate an effect size. Cohen (1977) provides rough guidelines of d = .2 (small effect), d = .5 (medium effect), and d = .8 (large effect), with the caveat that it is better to obtain these standards for comparison from the professional literature than to use these somewhat arbitrary guidelines. In fact, the methods used in meta-analysis have been used by Cohen (1977), Haase et al. (1982), and others to begin to develop such standards.

Interestingly, a 0.50 standard deviation improvement in achievement scores is considered to be a conventional measure of practical significance (Rossi and Wright, 1977). Similarly, the National Institute of Education's Joint Dissemination Review Panel observed that usually one-third ($0.33\,Sd_x$), but at times as small as one-fourth ($0.25\,Sd_x$), standard deviation improvement is considered to be educationally significant (Tallmadge, 1977).

Effect sizes reported in standard deviation units are often not readily interpretable nor well understood. Cohen (1977) provides a table for translating the effect size d into measures of nonoverlap, which Glass (1976, 1977) has introduced to the meta-analytic approach to reviewing research domains. In this approach, the average effect size is transformed into a graphical representation of the effect on the degree of overlap between the control and experimental groups. Cohen (1977) provides the percentiles of nonoverlap $U_3$ corresponding to various values of d in his text on power analysis, although values obtained from a normal distribution table are essentially equivalent to Cohen's $U_3$ tabled values. If we go to a normal curve table in any statistical text and look up the area under the curve associated with our d value, we will obtain the percentage of the experimental group which exceeds the upper half of cases for our control group population.

For example, the area under the normal curve associated with $d_{average} = 0.32$ is .625. This means that the average person receiving the exercise intervention would have a self-concept score greater than 62.5 percent of the people in the non-exercise control group. Thus exercise could be expected to move the typical person from the 50th to the 62.5th percentile of self-concept for the non-exercising population. This overlap between the two distributions is often presented graphically in order to enhance interpretation, as can be seen in Figure 1.

Other graphical methods that have been used to summarize effect sizes are illustrated in the following discussion for correlational relationships. These typically consist of developing a frequency distribution of the effect sizes included in the collection of studies that are synthesized.

## Correlational Relationships

The methods for synthesizing the results of correlational studies that report on the relationship between two variables, both measured on interval or ratio scales, are rather straightforward. Essentially, the average of the correlations between the two variables that examine the same research question across separate research studies is obtained. This is typically done by averaging the raw Pearson correlation coefficients (r) using formula 12 or transforming each r into its associated Z statistic using Fisher's r to Z transformation. These $Z_r$ s are then averaged using formula 13 and then transformed back to r. Typically $\bar{r}$ (mean r) and not $\bar{Z}_r$ (mean Fisher r) or $\bar{r}^2$ is used and reported as the effect size indicator.

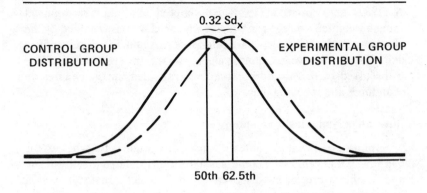

**CONTROL GROUP DISTRIBUTION**

0.32 Sd$_x$

**EXPERIMENTAL GROUP DISTRIBUTION**

50th 62.5th

PERCENTILE OF CONTROL GROUP DISTRIBUTION

Figure 1: Average Effect Size in Standard Deviation Units (SD$_x$)

$$\bar{r} = \frac{\Sigma r}{n} \qquad [12]$$

where r = Pearson correlation from each study and n = the number of correlation coefficients combined.

$$\bar{Z}_r = \frac{\Sigma Z_r}{n} \qquad [13]$$

where $Z_r$ = Fisher Z for each r and n = the number of correlation coefficients combined.

There is some discussion in the literature concerning the necessity of using the Fisher r to Z transformation in meta-analysis. Many investigators report both $\bar{r}$ and $\bar{Z}_r$ , and practically speaking the difference is small, although Schmidt, Hunter, and their colleagues (Hunter et al., 1982; Schmidt et al., 1980) have reported an instance where using the Fisher Z transformation resulted in a larger result (by about .07). Fisher (1932) noted that $Z_r$ tended to slightly overestimate the population r, but that the difference is negligible except when the sample size is small while the population r is large. The interested reader is referred to the discussion of this issue by Glass et al. (1981), Hunter et al. (1982), and Rosenthal (1984). Hunter et al. and others recommend using a weighted average r in which each correlation is weighted by the number of subjects in that particular study. Again, many researchers like to include this weighted mean along with the unweighted mean. This is discussed further, and an example is provided, in the chapter on examining and reducing bias.

## Illustrative Numerical Example

Suppose we wanted to review previous studies that tested the hypothesis that personal income was significantly related to self-esteem, and our literature review discovered only four fictitional studies that addressed this question. The results of these studies are summarized in Table 4.

Applying formula 12 to these four studies, we find

$$\bar{r} = \frac{.13 + .56 - .24 + .67}{4} = .28 \qquad [14]$$

Similarly, when formula 13 for Fisher's r to Z transformation is used, we find

$$\bar{Z}_r = \frac{.13 + .63 - .25 + .81}{4} = .33 \qquad [15]$$

When we transform a $\bar{Z}_r$ of .33 back to $\bar{r}$, we find that this results in r = .32, or .04 larger than the average of the raw correlation coefficients.

Often either frequency distributions or stem and leaf diagrams are used to summarize a large number of correlations found in a literature search. Suppose we found 15 studies reporting the following correlations (r) between personal income and self-esteem: .20, .17, .41, −.24, .27, .34, .37, −.06, .26, .67, .37, .23, .38, .35, and .40, respectively. A stem and leaf diagram (Tukey, 1977) similar to the one shown in Table 5 could be constructed to summarize the results of our meta-analysis of these 15 studies. For example, the largest of these 15 correlations, .67, would be depicted in our stem and leaf diagram in Table 5 by placing the first digit (.6) as the stem and the second digit (.07) as the leaf. The table is constructed to include stems for all values between the largest and smallest (−.24 in our example) correlations. Each correlation is then

TABLE 4

Correlations Between Personal Income and Self-Esteem
in Four Fictional Studies

| Study | $n$ | $r_{xy}$ | $Z_r$ |
|-------|-----|----------|-------|
| A | 16 | .13 | .13 |
| B | 82 | .56** | .63 |
| C | 102 | −.24* | −.25 |
| D | 47 | .67** | .81 |

*$p < .05$, two-tailed test; **$p < .01$, two-tailed test.

TABLE 5

Stem and Leaf Display of Fictional Correlations
Between Personal Income and Self-Esteem

| $r$ | | | | | | | Summary Statistics | |
|-----|---|---|---|---|---|---|--------------------|---|
| .6 | 7 | | | | | | | |
| .5 | | | | | | | Maximum r | .67 |
| .4 | 0 | 1 | | | | | Third quartile ($Q_3$) | .38 |
| .3 | 4 | 5 | 7 | 7 | 8 | | Median ($Q_2$) | .34 |
| .2 | 0 | 3 | 6 | 7 | | | First quartile ($Q_1$) | .20 |
| .1 | 7 | | | | | | Minimum r | −.24 |
| 0 | | | | | | | Mean ($\bar{r}$) | .27 |
| −.0 | 6 | | | | | | $Sd_{\bar{r}}$ | .21 |
| −.1 | | | | | | | Weighted mean | .28 |
| −.2 | 4 | | | | | | | |

included in the display in a similar manner as that described for .67. Measures of central tendency (e.g., mean, median, weighted mean) and variability (e.g., maximum, minimum, standard deviation) are typically included in a stem and leaf display to facilitate easier interpretation of the set of correlations.

## Interpreting Effect Sizes for Correlational Studies

The issues surrounding the interpretation of what constitutes a large effect for correlational studies are similar to those previously discussed for studies of group differences. It is always preferable to look to the research literature for evaluation standards like those provided by Haase et al. (1982) for counseling psychology research. In the absence of such standards, Cohen (1977) again provides rough guidelines for small ($r = .10$), medium ($r = .30$), and large ($r = .50$) effect sizes. Thus an average correlation of approximately .28 suggests a medium-sized effect for the relationship between personal income and self-esteem. Admittedly, these guidelines are somewhat arbitrary in nature. Keeping this arbitrariness in mind, however, they can be helpful in placing correlations within some interpretive context.

While not resolving the problem of interpretation of correlational effects, Rosenthal and Rubin (1982a) provide a more intuitive, insightful, and perhaps useful way to evaluate the practical importance of correlation coefficients. This procedure is based on the mathematical transformation of a correlation coefficient $(r)$ to chi square $(\chi^2)$ and provides what Rosenthal and Rubin (1982a) call a "binominal effect size display" (BESD) for $2 \times 2$ tables. The BESD is the estimated difference in success probabilities between treatment and control. Practically speaking, this transformation is simple to calculate and enables us to more easily interpret $r$ in terms of the effect on success or improvement rates attributable to treatment procedures. For example, in our fictitional study we found an average correlation of .28 for 15 studies of the relationship between personal income and self-esteem. This indicates that approximately 8 percent of the variability in self-esteem is associated with variability in personal income, with greater personal income associated with higher self-esteem. This 8 percent figure was obtained in the traditional fashion of using the square of the correlation coefficient as an estimate of the shared variance between the two variables that are correlated. In our example, $r^2 = (.28)^2 = .08$. Table 6 presents a correlation of .28 in terms of the BESD.

For the sake of illustration, if personal income were to be categorized as above and below the median level and self-esteem were categorized as positive or negative, a correlation of .28 would correspond to increasing the success rate (i.e., positive self-esteem) by 28 percent. Having above average personal income would be associated with an increase in the percentage of people with positive self-esteem from about 36 to 64 percent.

Table 7 provides a summary of the corresponding BESD values and changes in success rates associated with various values of $r$. From a practical perspective, it can be argued that a correlation of 0.2 or higher, which is based on a large enough sample to be statistically significant is meaningful, inasmuch as $r = 0.2$ translates into an improvement in success rate of from 40 to 60 percent. Certainly correlations of 0.3 and 0.4 are meaningful and relevant, particularly if based on results obtained from many studies with large numbers of representative subjects.

It is apparent from Table 7 that the improvement in success rate is equivalent to the magnitude of $r$. That is, a correlation of .28 translates

TABLE 6

Illustration of the Binomial Effect Size Display for
$\bar{r} = .28$ Between Personal Income and Self-Esteem

|  | Self-Esteem | | |
| Personal Income | Negative | Positive | Total |
| --- | --- | --- | --- |
| Below median level | 64 | 36 | 100 |
| Above median level | 36 | 64 | 100 |
| Total | 100 | 100 | 200 |

TABLE 7

Binomial Effect Size Displays for
Various Correlation Coefficients

| | Amount of Shared Variance | Success Rate Increased | |
| r | $r^2$ | From | To |
| --- | --- | --- | --- |
| .10 | .01 | .45 | .55 |
| .20 | .04 | .40 | .60 |
| .30 | .09 | .35 | .65 |
| .40 | .16 | .30 | .70 |
| .50 | .25 | .25 | .75 |
| .60 | .36 | .20 | .80 |
| .70 | .49 | .15 | .85 |
| .80 | .64 | .10 | .90 |
| .90 | .81 | .05 | .95 |

SOURCE: Adapted from Rosenthal and Rubin (1982a).
NOTE: The above success rates and any others associated with a specific r are calculated as follows: Success Rates $= .50 \pm \frac{r}{2}$.

into a 28 percent improvement (64 percent – 36 percent). These success rates are obtained from formula 15.

$$\text{Success rates} = 0.50 \pm \frac{r}{2} \qquad [16]$$

## Selecting a Common Metric

Often when reviewing the literature pertaining to a specific research question, the reviewer encounters studies using diverse research designs. Some studies may report results as differences between groups using t, F, or other statistics, while still other studies may report results as associations between variables using $\chi^2$, r, or other statistics. In order to conduct an empirical evaluation of this literature using meta-analytic procedures, it is necessary to convert all of these various summary statistics into a simple common metric or effect size in order to aggregate and synthesize them.

Perhaps the most common statistic or effect size measure selected for this purpose is the Pearson Product Moment Correlation r. An alternative procedure would be to convert these various summary statistics to the effect size index d. Guidelines for converting the most common test statistics to r and d are summarized in Tables 8 and 9, respectively. Cohen (1965, 1977), Friedman (1968), Glass et al. (1981), and Rosenthal (1984) discuss this procedure and provide guidelines for transforming other less common statistics.

Once either r or d is selected as the common metric to be used in the meta-analysis, each statistic is converted to this common metric and the results for each independent study are aggregated using the methods previously described.

## Mediating Effects

It is important to test whether third variables are mediators of the effect we are examining in our primary research hypothesis. That is, we could question whether gender, race, geographical location, year the research study was conducted, and so on mediated the relation between personal income and self-esteem in our fictitional example. Average effect sizes across studies could be calculated and evaluated for these potential mediating variable categories.

Suppose we had 150 fictitional studies and were able to obtain effect sizes from some of them for the categories listed in Table 10. Of the reported studies, 60 were either conducted with samples of females or the effect size for only females was provided or computed from information provided in the studies; likewise for the 120 studies averaged to obtain $\bar{r}$ for males only. The average effect size for females was .14 (SD = .19, n = 60), and for males it was .46 (SD = .21, n = 120). The effect size for each of these 180 samples could then be correlated with the gender of the samples, coding females = 0 and males = 1. Suppose this resulted in a correlation of .38 ($p < .01$, n = 180), which would indicate that stronger effect sizes tended to be obtained from male samples rather than female samples. That is, the relation between personal income and self-esteem tended to be stronger for males than for

**TABLE 8**
**Guidelines for Converting Various Test Statistics to r**

| Statistic to Be Converted | Formula for Transformation to r | Comment |
|---|---|---|
| t | $r = \sqrt{\dfrac{t^2}{t^2 + df}}$ | |
| F | $r = \sqrt{\dfrac{F}{F + df\,(error)}}$ | Use only for comparing two group means (i.e., numerator df = 1) |
| $\chi^2$ | $r = \sqrt{\dfrac{\chi^2}{n}}$ | n = sample size Use only for 2 x 2 frequency tables (df = 1) |
| d | $r = \dfrac{d}{\sqrt{d^2 + 4}}$ | |

**TABLE 9**
**Guidelines for Converting Various Test Statistics to d**

| Statistic to Be Converted | Formula for Transformation to d | Comment |
|---|---|---|
| t | $d = \dfrac{2t}{\sqrt{df}}$ | |
| F | $d = \dfrac{2\sqrt{F}}{\sqrt{df(error)}}$ | Use only for comparing two group means (i.e., numerator df = 1) |
| r | $d = \dfrac{2r}{\sqrt{1 - r^2}}$ | |

TABLE 10

Average Effect Size ($\bar{r}$) for Subgroupings of Characteristics
of 150 Fictional Studies of the Relation Between
Personal Income and Self-Esteem

| Characteristic | $\bar{r}$ | $SD\bar{r}$ | Number of Studies |
|---|---|---|---|
| Gender | | | |
| females | .14 | .19 | 60 |
| males | .46 | .21 | 120 |
| Race | | | |
| black | .29 | .18 | 30 |
| white | .28 | .15 | 90 |

females. Effect sizes are often regressed on a number of potential
mediating variables using multiple linear regression techniques. Glass et
al. (1981) and Hedges and Olkin (1983b, 1985) provide more detailed
discussions of this approach.

An alternative strategy for examining a mediating effect would be to
directly test the significance of the difference between the two effect
sizes, .14 for females and .46 for males in our example. This could be
done by using formula 16 to test the difference between two independent
correlations.

$$Z = \frac{Z_{\bar{r}1} - Z_{\bar{r}2}}{\sqrt{\dfrac{1}{N_1 - 3} + \dfrac{1}{N_2 - 3}}} \qquad [17]$$

where $Z_{\bar{r}1}$ and $Z_{\bar{r}2}$ = Fisher's r to Z transformation for the two $\bar{r}$s, and $N_1$
and $N_2$ = the number of studies that the $\bar{r}$ s are based on.

In our example, $\bar{r}$'s of .14 and .46 equal $Z_{\bar{r}}$s of .141 and .497,
respectively, and we find

$$Z = \frac{.141 - .497}{\sqrt{\dfrac{1}{60 - 3} + \dfrac{1}{120 - 3}}} = \frac{-.356}{.162} = -2.20 \qquad [18]$$

Thus the difference between the average effect sizes for males and
females is statistically significant ($p < .01$).

A similar approach can be taken if the average d rather than the average r is used as the indicator of effect size across studies. That is, d for females and males, respectively, is calculated, and the d for each sample is correlated with gender, with females again coded as 0 and males as 1. Alternately, the differences between $\bar{d}$ s for males and females could be statistically tested using the procedures discussed by Hedges (1982a) and Rosenthal and Rubin (1982b). A formula for making this comparison and an example are provided in the discussion of tests of the homogeneity of effects in the following chapter.

## 4. EXAMINING AND REDUCING BIAS

There are many ways in which an individual piece of research or review of research literature, whether of a qualitative or quantitative nature, can lead to erroneous or biased analyses or conclusions. Some of the ways that biased conclusions may be obtained in a meta-analysis include the effects of a strong bias toward publishing positive but not negative results; weighing equally the results of all studies examining the same research question, even though there may be qualitative differences among them; including multiple tests of a hypothesis from a single study; and not ensuring a high level of agreement or reliability among raters in the coding of study characteristics, whether substantive or methodological. Each of these issues presents difficult and often subtle problems for the meta-analyst. While strategies for approaching these difficulties have been proposed, the final word on many of these issues is still out. At the same time, many advances have been made since meta-analysis was suggested as an approach to quantitatively reviewing research literature.

### Fail-Safe N and File Drawer Problem

It is unlikely that a literature review will uncover every study of a hypothesis that has been conducted. Rosenthal (1979) has called this the "file drawer problem" because of the tendency for studies supporting the null hypothesis of no significant results to be more likely to be buried away in file drawers. Kraemer and Andrews (1982: 405) note: "Published research studies tend to be biased toward positive findings. A study is often abandoned if it is apparent that statistically significant findings will not be forthcoming. Reports of nonsignificant findings are generally unpublishable even when they are replications of earlier studies reporting significant results." Even if investigators submit results of these studies for publication, it is generally difficult for editors to publish them because of the many studies they receive with statistically significant results. This may enhance the likelihood of a type I publication bias error in finding more positive results than is really the case were all studies to be located and included in our review.

Many meta-analysts perform separate analyses for published and unpublished studies (presented at professional meetings or located in retrieval systems for unpublished papers such as ERIC, Dissertation Abstracts International, and the like) and test for differences in effect size according to the source of the study. Rosenthal addressed this problem analytically by suggesting that we calculate the number of studies confirming the null hypothesis that would be needed to reverse a conclusion that a significant relationship exists. Cooper (1979) called this the Fail Safe N ($N_{fs}$) for the number of additional studies in a meta-analysis that would be necessary to reverse the overall probability obtained from our combined test to a value higher than our critical value for statistical significance, usually .05 or .01.

Formula 19 can be used to compute $N_{fs}$ for p = .05, while formula 20 is used for $p$ = .01.

$$N_{fs.05} = \left(\frac{\Sigma Z}{1.645}\right)^2 - N \qquad [19]$$

$$N_{fs.01} = \left(\frac{\Sigma Z}{2.33}\right)^2 - N \qquad [20]$$

where $\Sigma Z$ = the sum of individual Z scores and N = the number of studies combined using the Stouffer combined significance test procedure.

If we apply equation 19 to our example of the four fictitious studies in Table 2 testing the hypothesis that exercise positively affects self-concept, we obtain the following result:

$$N_{fs.05} = \left(\frac{2.65 - 1.88 + 1.98 + 1.52}{1.645}\right)^2 - 4 \qquad [21]$$

$$= \left(\frac{4.27}{1.645}\right)^2 - 4 = 6.75 - 4 = 2.75$$

Thus we need approximately three studies, each showing no effect (i.e., Z = 0.0) or summing to no effect (i.e., $\Sigma$ Z = 0) to reverse our conclusion that exercise positively influences self-concept at $p$ = .05. Orwin (1983) has provided an analogous fail-safe N for the average effect size $\overline{d}$ that can be obtained using equation 22.

$$N_{fs} = \frac{N(\overline{d} - \overline{d}_c)}{\overline{d}_c} \qquad [22]$$

where N = the number of studies in the meta-analysis, $\overline{d}$ = the average effect size for the studies synthesized, and $\overline{d}_c$ = the criterion value selected that $\overline{d}$ would equal when some knowable number of hypothetical studies ($N_{fs}$) were added to the meta-analysis.

When calculating the fail-safe N for statistical significance based on the Stouffer combined test, traditionally agreed upon criterion p values of .05 and .01 are typically used. Because of the lack of formally agreed upon criterion d values for effect size, Orwin (1983) suggests using Cohen's (1977) suggestion of d = .2 (small effect), d = .5 (medium effect), and d = .8 (large effect). When we select d = .2 as our criterion value ($\overline{d}_c$), we find that we would need only about two or three additional studies exhibiting a small enough effect to bring down our average to .2 for our $\overline{d}$ = 0.32 obtained in our meta-analysis of our four fictitional studies in Table 3. This can be shown from equation 23.

$$N_{fs.2} = \frac{(4)(0.32 - 0.20)}{.20} = 2.4 \qquad [23]$$

**Weighting Studies by Sample Size**

It can be argued that not all studies synthesized in a meta-analytic literature review should be given equal weight. Some studies may be based on very small or unrepresentative samples of subjects, while others may use more elegant randomized control group designs with large numbers of subjects. To give these studies equal weight may not be intuitively pleasing and could lead to the less representative studies contributing just as much weight to the results of our meta-analysis as the more well-designed studies. Mosteller and Bush (1954) suggest weighting each of the standard normal deviates (Zs) used for the Stouffer combined test by the size of the sample on which it is based.

This is typically done by using the df associated with each statistical test used in the meta-analysis according to formula 24.

$$\text{weighted } Z_c = \frac{\Sigma \, df \, Z}{\sqrt{\Sigma df^2}} \qquad [24]$$

where $Z$ = the standard normal deviate associated with the one-tailed $p$ value for each statistic synthesized and df = the degrees of freedom associated with the statistic. In our example of four fictitional studies in Table 2, we would obtain the following weighted $Z_c$:

$$\text{weighted } Z_c = \frac{(80)(2.65) + (60)(-1.88) + (200)(1.98) + (20)(1.52)}{\sqrt{(80)^2 + (60)^2 + (200)^2 + (20)^2}} \qquad [25]$$

$$\text{weighted } Z_c = \frac{525.6}{224.5} = 2.34$$

The probability of obtaining this value of (weighted) $Z_c$ or larger is $p$ $(Z \geq 2.34) < .010$, one-tailed. These results may be compared with those obtained earlier for the unweighted $Z_c$ of 2.13 ($p < .017$, one-tailed) for these four studies from equation 6. Because the sample size was greatest for Study C, the unweighted $Z_c$ changed to a weighted $Z_c$ in the direction of the results for this study. While the difference between unweighted $Z_c$ = 2.13 and weighted $Z_c$ = 2.34 is not very large in our example, this is not always the case. In the unweighted case, many studies with small samples that contain results inconsistent with most studies in a meta-analysis could exert a much stronger influence on the results than warranted. In general, it is recommended that both the weighted and unweighted $Z_c$ be calculated, and many meta-analytic studies report both values.

## Unbiased Estimate of Effect Size

Hedges (1982a) and Rosenthal and Rubin (1982b) have presented methods for obtaining an unbiased estimate of the effect size d. Hedges (1981) developed the sampling distribution of d and showed that d is a slightly biased estimate of effect size. Hedges (1982a) has shown that a weighted estimator of effect size is asymptomatically efficient and quite accurate when experimental and control group sample sizes are greater than 10 and effect sizes (d) are less than about 1.5, which is the case in most instances. Formula 26 can be used to obtain this weighted $\bar{d}$:

$$\bar{d} = \frac{\Sigma wd}{\Sigma w} \qquad [26]$$

where d is the unweighted effect size and w is the reciprocal of the estimated variance of d in each of the studies to be aggregated in the meta-analysis. Both Hedges (1982a) and Rosenthal and Rubin (1982b) provide formulae for calculating this variance estimate. In instances where the experimental and control group sample sizes are approximately equal and greater than 10, Rosenthal and Rubin (1982c) provide the formula below to estimate w for each independent study:

$$w = \frac{2N}{8 + d^2} \qquad [27]$$

where d = unweighted effect size and N = total sample size in the study for both the experimental and control groups.

For example, for Study A, previously summarized in Tables 2 and 3, we can obtain the following estimate for w from equation 27.

$$w = \frac{2(82)}{8 + (.60)^2} = 19.6 \qquad [28]$$

Estimates for w for studies B, C, and D were obtained in the same fashion and are summarized in Table 11 for convenience. We can then proceed to obtain our unbiased, weighted average d for our four studies according to equation 26.

$$\bar{d} = \frac{(19.6)(.60) + (15.0)(-.50) + (49.4)(.43) + (5.1)(.75)}{19.6 + 15.0 + 49.4 + 5.1} \qquad [29]$$

$$\bar{d} = \frac{29.33}{89.1} = 0.33$$

TABLE 11
Results of Four Fictional Studies Used
to Obtain a Weighted, Unbiased $\bar{d}$

| Study | N | d | w |
|-------|-----|-------|------|
| A | 82 | 0.60 | 19.6 |
| B | 62 | −0.50 | 15.0 |
| C | 202 | 0.43 | 49.4 |
| D | 22 | 0.75 | 5.1 |

NOTE: w is calculated from equation 27.

Thus our unbiased, weighted $\bar{d}$ of 0.33 is a little larger than the unweighted d of 0.32 obtained in equation 11. As a practical matter, Green and Hall (1984) note that this correction factor for the slight bias of d is too near unity to make much of a difference when the sample size (n) for a study is greater than 10 subjects.

## Tests of Homogeneity

Increasing numbers of meta-analytic syntheses are being reported as this approach to quantitatively reviewing a research domain has become more widely known. Hedges, Oklin, and others have begun to address the underlying statistical theory for these methods, which has lagged behind the application of the methods. Some of these issues are not only of theoretical interest but can be very helpful in providing practical guidance in the implementation of a meta-analysis. Such is the case for tests of homogeneity.

In our original example in Table 1, we wanted to synthesize the results of studies A, B, C, and D in order to test the hypothesis that exercise can lead to a more positive self-concept. In order to quantitatively synthesize all of these studies in one meta-analysis, it is assumed that each study provides a sample estimate of the size of effect that is representative of the population effect size. If a series of independent studies provide a common (homogeneous) estimate of the population effect size, then it is more likely that the various studies are testing the same hypothesis. If these estimates are heterogeneous, then the question of whether each study is testing the same hypothesis arises. Heterogeneity provides a warning that it may not be appropriate to combine and synthesize all the study results in one meta-analysis. The investigator would need to consider whether to conduct separate meta-analytic syntheses for different subsets of studies, each of which represent homogeneous results.

Hedges (1982a) discusses the situation in which a treatment produces statistically significant large positive effects in half of the studies and statistically significant large negative effects in the other half. Each of the studies has significantly large effects, yet the overall effect would lead to the misleading conclusion that the overall effect of treatment was zero were they to be aggregated together in one meta-analysis. Hedges's example illustrates how misleading the aggregation of a set of heterogeneous studies would be in this instance.

While this extreme scenario may or may not be very likely, a practical problem in any meta-analysis is whether or not to include a particular study in the collection of studies to be aggregated and synthesized. This point is addresssed further in the discussion of issues of validity and reliability, but the methods provided in this section can be used to test for the homogeneity of studies to help identify those which represent outliers. These studies should be examined in order to understand what may cause them to be different. Graphing the frequency distribution of effect sizes for the studies synthesized is very helpful in this regard. Light and Pillemer (1984) provide many helpful suggestions for interpreting these types of graphical results. It is possible that it may be necessary to treat outlier studies separately, perhaps in a separate meta-analysis.

There is still some debate concerning what to do with the results of independent studies when their results are found to be significantly heterogenous. Hedges (1982a) and Hunter et al. (1982) suggest that it is inappropriate to include them in one meta-analysis. Harris and Rosenthal (1985) argue that heterogeneity is analogous to individual differences among subjects within single studies and is common whenever many studies by different investigators using different methods are examined. Light and Pillemer (1984) believe that these differences, and the studies identified as outliers, should be capitalized upon through close examination to develop increased understanding and new hypotheses. Even Hedges (Becker and Hedges, 1984) has admitted: "It is not necessarily inadvisable to draw inferences from heterogeneous effects."

## Homogeneity of Statistical Tests

Rosenthal (1983, 1984) provides statistical tests to assess the homogeneity/heterogeneity of the standard normal deviates Z corresponding to the one-tailed $p$ values from the studies we want to combine. Extended tables of the $t$ distribution are often needed to obtain these one-tailed $p$ values and may be found in Rosenthal and

Rosnow (1984) or Federighi (1959). In the case of comparing the results from just two studies, the procedure is rather straightforward and is provided in formula 30.

$$Z = \frac{Z_1 - Z_2}{\sqrt{2}} \qquad [30]$$

The difference between $Z_1$ and $Z_2$ is distributed as $Z$ when divided by $\sqrt{2}$.

For example, suppose we want to test whether the result of study A ($Z = 2.65$) is significantly different from the results of study B ($Z = -1.88$) as previously reported in Table 2. We would obtain the following result:

$$Z = \frac{(2.65) - (-1.88)}{\sqrt{2}} = 3.20 \qquad [31]$$

Our resultant $Z$ of 3.20 has a $p$ value of $< .001$, one-tailed, or $< .002$, two-tailed. The implication is that we need to explore why the results of these two studies are different. We may not want to include both of them in the same meta-analysis.

There may be several plausible explanations why these two studies are significantly different in our example. First, the two studies used different measures to assess self-concept. Study A used the Coopersmith measure, while Study B used the Tennessee measure developed for children. Results from the two studies could differ if the samples of subjects for the two studies differ widely—for example, if study A was conducted with college students or adults while study B included younger children. Additionally, there could be a vast array of design or methodological differences between the studies. Ideally, most of these study characteristics would be coded as described previously in the discussion of mediating effects. Analysis of these substantive or methodological characteristics would be imperative. Alternatively, we could conduct separate meta-analyses for studies with samples of adults and children, respectively (or for any other characteristic difference between studies).

In the instance where we desire to test the homogeneity/heterogeneity of more than two independent studies, an overall or omnibus test, or what Rosenthal (1983) calls a diffuse test, must be used to examine whether the group of studies is homogeneous or not. If these studies exhibit significant heterogeneity, then it is imperative to examine the outliers in the distribution of studies and to test for mediating effects that may contribute to the heterogeneity. Equation 32 may be used for this overall diffuse test.

$$\chi^2 = \Sigma(Z - \overline{Z})^2 \qquad [32]$$

with degrees of freedom (df) = K – 1 where K = the number of Zs from independent studies. Turning again to our example in Table 2, we can test the homogeneity of the Zs associated with these four studies, 2.65 (Study A), –1.88 (Study B), 1.98 (Study C), and 1.52 (Study D).

$$\chi^2 = (2.65 - 1.07)^2 + (-1.88 - 1.07)^2 + \qquad [33]$$

$$(1.98 - 1.07)^2 + (1.52 - 1.07)^2 = 12.23$$

A $\chi^2$ value of 12.23 with K – 1 = 4 – 1 = 3 df is significant at $p < .01$, indicating that our four studies are significantly heterogeneous. In order to explore what is causing this heterogeneity, it would be reasonable to focus on study B, in which a result inconsistent with the direction of results in the other studies was found.

### Homogeneity of Effect Size

We can test for the homogeneity/heterogeneity of effect sizes in an analogous manner to testing for the homogeneity of statistical tests described in the previous section. Equation 34 may be used for this purpose (Rosenthal and Rubin, 1982b, 1982c):

$$\chi^2 = \Sigma(w(d - \overline{d})^2) \qquad [34]$$

where $\overline{d}$ is the weighted mean d of the studies to be aggregated, d is the effect size for each study, and w is the reciprocal of the estimated variance of each d. This results in a $\chi^2$ distribution with K – 1 df where K = the number of studies. Weighted $\overline{d}$ and w may be obtained from formulae 26 and 27 as previously described, where N = the total sample size in the study.

For our example using studies A, B, C, and D in Table 11, we obtain the following result with equation 34 and $\overline{d}$ = .33 obtained from equation 29.

$$\chi^2 = (19.6)(.60 - .33)^2 + (15.0)(-.50 - .33)^2 + \qquad [35]$$

$$(49.4)(.43 - .33)^2 + (5.1)(.75 - .33)^2$$

$$= 14.44$$

With df = K – 1 = 4 – 1 = 3, a $\chi^2$ value of 14.4 has a $p < .001$. This indicates significant heterogeneity among the effect sizes obtained from the four independent studies. Again, we would want to focus on Study B to try to see why it is different from the other three studies.

## Studies with More Than One Statistic

Many studies may provide more than one test of significance relevant to the hypothesis that a meta-analysis is examining. Glass and his colleagues (Smith and Glass, 1980; Glass et al., 1981) have included multiple tests from the same study in a single meta-analysis, while other meta-analysts do not (e.g., Kulik et al., 1980; Mazzuca, 1982; Findley and Cooper, 1983; Steinkamp and Maehr, 1983; Harris and Rosenthal, 1985).

Kulik (1983) argues that including multiple results from a single study inflates the sample size of statistical tests and effects beyond the number of independent studies. While this may increase the power of our meta-analysis, it becomes difficult to determine the amount of error in statistics describing the collection of results to be synthesized. Kulik (1983), Rosenthal (1984), and others recommend performing separate meta-analyses for each type of dependent variable rather than lumping different types of outcome measures in a single analysis. Mazzuca (1982), for example, treated the effects of patient education on compliance with a therapeutic regimen, on physiological progress, and on long-range health outcomes in individual meta-analyses. Similarly, Harris and Rosenthal (1985) report the results of separate meta-analyses for each of 31 behavior categories of interpersonal expectancy effects. Kulik et al. (1980) examined the effects of computer-based teaching on achievement, attitudes, and study time separately within one quantitative review. Kulik (1983) maintains that lumping these various outcomes together would create conceptual confusion. Rosenthal (1984) suggests that at the least the effect of the independent variable should be examined on each of the various categories of dependent variables to understand which may be affected most and least. Trying to understand differential effects for different outcome measures may help to provide insight for future theory and practice.

Several other approaches have been taken for this problem of multiple dependent variables (or the nonindependence of effects from the same study). Steinkamp and Maehr (1983), for example, included all correlational results from the same studies in one meta-analysis but also calculated a mean effect size correlation based on the average correlation from each independent study. They then went on to do a series of further meta-analyses to examine the magnitude of effects for conceptual subcategories of interest. In yet another approach to the problem, Gilbert et al. (1977) restricted to two the number of results from a single study in their meta-analysis.

Conducting separate meta-analyses for different classes of outcome dependent variables addressing the hypothesis of interest is a practical solution to the "apples and oranges" criticism of meta-analysis. This approach enhances the conceptual clarity and interpretation of the results of a meta-analysis as each category of outcome or dependent variable is examined in a separate meta-analytic synthesis. Thus apples are treated as apples and oranges as oranges.

Strube (1985) warns that meta-analysts should avoid averaging results within a study that would preclude analytical examination of the differences and similarities of results for different categories of outcomes. The interested reader is referred to Strube (1985) for an exact computational procedure for adjusting the Stouffer combined test to accommodate nonindependent hypotheses tests. His procedure may result in a more conservative combined test than merely including all nonindependent results from the same studies for the reasons discussed above. Using nonindependent results in one analysis would tend to inflate the Type I error rate for the meta-analysis and should thus be avoided. Tracz et al. (1985) demonstrate a multiple linear regression approach to meta-analysis that takes into consideration multiple treatments, nonindependence, interaction, and covariance by building full and restricted models. By dummy coding study vectors with 1's if an effect size came from a study, and 0's otherwise, they demonstrated how the general linear model can be used for identifying the correct degrees of freedom and error terms when there is dependency in the data. This issue of nonindependence or multiple dependent variables is complex and important, and is just beginning to be addressed more sophisticatedly.

## Validity and Reliability Issues

A number of articles have studied or commented on reliability issues in meta-analysis (e.g., Glass et al., 1981; Green and Hall, 1984; Hunter et al., 1982; McGuire et al., 1985; Orwin and Cordray, 1985; Rosenthal, 1984; Stock et al., 1982). When conducting a meta-analysis, it is necessary to consider the reliability (consistency) of locating research results. How likely is it for independent meta-analysts to locate and include the same studies? How comprehensive is the collection of studies? Meta-analytic results may be affected if this is not a highly consistent process.

Another critical issue is the degree of reliability in coding the features of studies to be included in the analysis. Stock et al. (1982) and Rosenthal (1984) provide summaries of the degree of interrater reliability obtained from coding different study characteristics. Stock et al. (1982) offer seven suggestions for enhancing intercoder reliability:

(1) develop and pilot-test coding forms before coding characteristics for the meta-analysis;

(2) develop a detailed, explicit codebook that is keyed to the coding forms;

(3) provide coder training based on both the codebook and coding forms;

(4) measure and report intercoder reliability as part of the meta-analysis;

(5) revise the codebook and forms and retrain coders as needed;

(6) develop procedures for adding new coders; and

(7) encourage coder involvement in discussions and decisions concerning coding rules.

Another reliability issue is the degree of consistency in the calculating and recording of the significance levels and effect size estimates of studies. Many of these outcome results are not reported directly in the primary studies, and the possibility of errors in their calculations and coding needs to be minimized.

Hunter et al. (1982) provide methods for adjusting for the unrelia-
bility of measures (correction for attenuation) and restriction of range,
both at the level of individual studies, and sampling error for the
collection of studies in the meta-analysis. Both Rosenthal (1984) and
Green and Hall (1984) believe these procedures to be burdensome and
overly restrictive and suggest always reporting uncorrected effect sizes
(correlations) when these adjustments are made and/or to look for
correlates (mediators) of effect sizes in lieu of these procedures. Linn
and Hastings (1984), Mabe and West (1982), Peters et al. (1985), and
Schmidt et al. (1980) provide examples of meta-analyses using the
procedures described by Hunter et al. (1982).

Wortman (1983) comments on issues concerning the external,
construct, internal, and statistical conclusion validities of meta-analysis.
External and construct validity both relate to the "apples" and
"oranges" problem of trying to determine which studies appropriately
belong in the collection of studies to be aggregated. Coding characteristics of studies and looking for mediating effects and testing the
homogeneity of the results (as previously discussed) are helpful in
examining and enhancing external validity in this regard.

Internal validity in meta-analysis is concerned with whether varia-
tions in design quality influence the outcomes of meta-analysis. This
factor should also be coded in the meta-analysis and empirically
examined. Some studies have found higher quality studies (i.e., larger
sample sizes, well-controlled sampling, and the like) to result in lower
effect sizes than poorer quality studies, while other meta-analyses have
shown design quality to be unrelated to effect size. Glass (1983: 401)
observes "as a general rule, there is seldom much more than one-tenth
standard deviation difference between average effects for high-validity
and low-validity experiments." Nevertheless, he notes that "it is
desirable for each meta-analysis to include an empirical examination of
internal validity." Such an empirical examination is desirable in each
meta-analysis in order to determine the degree of internal validity for
that particular set of studies. Green and Hall (1984) suggest that degree
of experimenter blindness, randomization, sample size, controls for
recording errors or cheating, type of dependent variable (e.g., self-report
versus objective), and publication bias are areas of methodological and
design quality that a good meta-analysis should examine.

## 5. NONPARAMETRIC METHODS

Interest in nonparametric measures of effect size has been growing since Glass et al. (1981) discussed various approaches to estimating effect sizes from nonparametric statistics and ordinal and dichotomous data. Use of a nonparametric estimator of effect size may be desirable when we have skewed, non-normal data or when some of the observations are outliers. Kraemer and Andrews (1982) point out limitations of the parametric effect size d, which include the view that the interpretation of d depends on an implicit assumption that control group scores are normally distributed, that the treatment benefits all subjects equally (the additivity assumption), and that d is not invariant under all monotonic transformations of scales (such as a log transformation).

One approach to handling this problem would be to transform our data in order to make it more normally distributed or to eliminate the outliers before conducting the meta-analysis with the parametric procedures previously described. Another approach would be to obtain the standard normal deviate (Z) associated with an accurate $p$ value associated with a nonparametric statistic reported for a study result. Still another approach would be to use the median in lieu of or in addition to the mean as our measure of central tendency as a descriptor of effect size. Several meta-analysts (e.g., Hyde, 1981; Mazzuca, 1982) have reported the median effect sizes for the collection of studies that were synthesized. In these instances, the effect size from each study that is included in the synthesis is still based on the difference between group means, the parametric effect size d. Kraemer and Andrews (1982) suggest using a nonparametric effect size based on the median from each study in the synthesis of the collection of studies. Rosenthal (1984: 34) warns, however, that "the use of medians in meta-analytic work tends to give results consistently favoring type II errors, i.e., results leading to estimates favoring the null hypothesis." The following discussion is based on work stimulated by Kraemer and Andrews (Hedges and Olkin, 1984; Krauth, 1983; Kraemer, 1984). Other approaches discussed by Glass et al. (1981), Katz et al. (1985), and Hodges and Lehman (1962) are recommended to those interested in examining further the issue of nonparametric effect size.

### Nonparametric Effect Size

The nonparametric effect size D for each study may be obtained from equation 36.

$$D = \Phi^{-1}(p) \qquad [36]$$

where D is a standard normal deviate, $\Phi^{-1}$ is the inverse of the cumulative standard normal distribution function, and p is the proportion of the control group subjects whose values on the dependent variable are less than the median value for the experimental group. Because it is possible for p to have values of 0 or 1 when the sample size (n) is small, Kraemer and Andrews (1982) recommend defining p as $1/(n + 1)$ when p = 0 and as $n/(n + 1)$ when p = 1 in order to avoid extreme effect sizes.

### Illustrative Numerical Example

The following example should help us in understanding how D is calculated from equation 36. Suppose we want to calculate the nonparametric effect size D for the impact of an exercise program on low self-esteem children. Our sample of 40 children in Table 12 was randomly assigned to experimental and control groups and asked to complete the Tennessee Self-Concept Scale after the experimental group had received the exercise intervention. If we examine the scores for the control group in Table 12, we see that 18 of the 20 children had scores less than 154.5, the median score of the experimental group. Our p = 18/20 = .90. Applying equation 36 to our data, we obtain the following result:

$$D = \Phi^{-1}(.90) = 1.28 \qquad [37]$$

The value for D is obtained from a standard normal curve table by selecting the Z (1.28, in this instance) associated with an area under the curve of .90.

The nonparametric effect size D may then be compared with the parametric effect size d obtained by using equation 8:

$$d = \frac{|\bar{x}_1 - \bar{x}_2|}{Sd} \qquad [8]$$

For our example in Table 12, we find that d = 1.17:

$$d = \frac{|135 - 154|}{16.3} = 1.17 \qquad [38]$$

**TABLE 12**
**Hypothetical Results of Self-Esteem Scores**
**for Two Groups of Children**

|        | Control Group (n = 20) | Experimental Group (n = 20) |
|--------|-----------------------|------------------------------|
|        | 130 | 130 |
|        | 131 | 131 |
|        | 135 | 144 |
|        | 136 | 146 |
|        | 136 | 128 |
|        | 138 | 156 |
|        | 124 | 161 |
|        | 126 | 162 |
|        | 104 | 160 |
|        | 142 | 131 |
|        | 114 | 158 |
|        | 166 | 166 |
|        | 153 | 150 |
|        | 169 | 186 |
|        | 127 | 188 |
|        | 130 | 153 |
|        | 120 | 144 |
|        | 121 | 147 |
|        | 149 | 169 |
|        | 150 | 170 |
| Mean   | 135 | 154 |
| Sd     | 16.3 | 17.0 |
| Median | 133 | 154.5 |

Thus we find our nonparametric effect size to be slightly larger than our parametric effect size, reflecting the skewness of the data.

The closer the skew of the data is to zero (i.e., normally distributed), the more similar the nonparametric effect size is to the parametric effect size. Kraemer and Andrews (1982) suggest that both parametric and non-parametric effect sizes be computed. While individual investigators can easily do this with their own studies, as a practical matter it is difficult for the meta-analyst to obtain the raw data for each study necessary to calculate the nonparametric effect size from published results for which this information is not provided.

When pooling the nonparametric effect sizes from independent studies, Kraemer and Andrews (1982) suggest weighting these effect sizes by their accompanying sample sizes as is done when pooling (i.e., averaging) parametric effect sizes according to equation 26. Kraemer and Andrews provide formulae for pretest/posttest, and pre-post/ control-experimental group studies, while Hedges and Olkin (1984) extend their work by providing formulae for other nonparametric estimators of effect size, including the control-experimental group formula 36 used in the present discussion.

## 6. SUMMARY AND CONCLUSIONS

Any statistical procedure or analytic approach can be misused or abused. As Green and Hall (1984: 52) aptly state: "Data analysis is an aid to thought, not a substitute." Most of the criticisms of quantitative approaches to reviewing the literature are objections to the misuse or abuse, real or potential, of meta-analysis. Following is a summary of some of the limitations and strengths of meta-analysis, as well as a series of guidelines for practice.

### Limitations of Meta-Analysis

A number of problems in conducting a quantitative review have been pointed out. Meta-analysts have developed a number of ways to analytically approach many of these problems, and all of the problems merit the thoughtful attention of the quantitative reviewer. Some of these issues are not analytical but conceptual in nature.

Meta-analysis has been accused of oversimplifying the results of a research domain by focusing on overall effects and downplaying mediating or interaction effects. The better examples of meta-analyses built potential mediating factors into their designs rather than ignorning them. They do this by coding the characteristics of studies to empirically examine whether such interactions exist. In practice many meta-analyses do not provide sufficient attention to possible interaction effects. One of the most difficult problems, however, is to identify which characteristics or properties of studies might mediate the relationship of interest. As Glass (1983) points out, there is no systematic logical procedure to identify these characteristics.

As a result of the judgments and decisions that the meta-analyst necessarily must make regarding which studies are appropriate to include in a quantitative review, meta-analysis has been criticized for mixing studies that measure "apples" with those that measure "oranges" so that no meaningful result can be obtained. While this is one of the first and most common criticisms of meta-analysis, a good meta-analysis capitalizes on this by coding apples as apples and oranges as oranges in order to empirically test whether and how they are similar or different (Green and Hall, 1984). Rather than ignore the possible impact of study quality on the results of a review (another frequent criticism), a good meta-analysis also will empirically examine this by coding and analyzing study quality.

Because of the elaborate coding system that must be developed for systematically conducting a meta-analysis, combined with the fact that many studies do not provide all the information necessary for it to be included in the analyses, there are many opportunities to make mistakes in the classification of studies or in calculating effect sizes. How to deal with multiple results within a single study remains a difficult issue that each meta-analyst must confront. The nonindependence of these results may make significance testing and the estimation of effect sizes problematic.

Perhaps one of the greatest dangers is conducting a quantitative review when the collection of available studies for a particular research domain are few in number and their results heterogeneous (Cook and Leviton, 1980). Whether they can reasonably be considered a sample of any domain becomes a critical question. The whole issue of the homogeneity/heterogeneity of results remains a difficult one. While there are analytical methods to determine the degree of heterogeneity, there is disagreement on exactly what to do should the results of the collection of studies be significantly heterogeneous.

Finally, the application of quantitative methods to literature reviews has proceeded more rapidly than the development of the statistical theory that underlies many of these methods. Hedges, Olkin, Kraemer, and others have begun to describe the statistical theory and models to which aggregated data can be fitted.

## Strengths of Meta-Analysis

Quantitative reviewing has been viewed as an efficient way to summarize large literatures (Green and Hall, 1984). It is often possible to reach stronger conclusions because more studies can be analyzed with statistical methods than in impressionistic literary review. Often this can bring effects into sharper focus, particularly when the results of all the studies are not consistent. Meta-analysis does not a priori prejudge and exclude some studies as unworthy because of their particular research designs, however weak. By empirically examining the effects of research quality on study findings, meta-analysis is likely to be more objective than traditional literary reviews.

Glass (1983) states that meta-analysis is evaluative and atheoretical, with an aim of assessing costs and benefits rather than explanation. This may be too modest a statement, however, as Light and Pillemer (1984), Green and Hall (1984), and others find meta-analysis helpful in highlighting gaps in the literature, providing insight into new directions for research, and finding mediating or interactional relationships or trends either too subtle to see or that cannot be hypothesized and tested in individual studies. While many critics believe the heterogeneity of findings to be damaging to a meta-analysis, others believe that the identification of outliers in meta-analysis deserves special attention and can lead to increased understanding and new hypotheses.

## Guidelines for Practice

The following guidelines are intended to be helpful in confronting the potential limitations and in capitalizing on the particular strengths of conducting a quantitative review.

(1) Define and report criteria for the inclusion and exclusion of studies. This is largely a substantive, conceptual issue, but quantitative issues such as how to handle a study with missing or incomplete data may also arise.

(2) Search for unpublished studies in order to test for a type I error publication bias.

(3) Develop coding categories to accommodate the largest proportion of the literature identified. It is better to code too many rather than too few characteristics of studies. Both substantive and methodological characteristics need to be coded, such as type and length of the intervention, sample characteristics, research design characteristics and quality, source of study (e.g., published, dissertation, internal report, and the like), date of study, and so on.

(4) Examine multiple independent and dependent variables separately through blocking, mediating effects. Look for interactions with the principal relationship being reviewed.

(5) Examine and graph the distribution of results and look for outliers to examine more closely. Test for the heterogeneity of results.

(6) Check the reliability of the raters who code the characteristics of studies.

(7) Always accompany combined tests of significance with estimates of effect size.

(8) Calculate both raw (unadjusted) and weighted combined tests and effect sizes to empirically examine the impact of sample size on results.

(9) Consider whether it is important and/or practical to calculate nonparametric as well as parametric effect size estimates.

(10) Consult the literature on meta-analysis for guidance when in doubt. Examine how others have approached particular problems in their quantitative reviews.

(11) Combine qualitative reviewing with quantitative reviewing. Examine the comparability of treatment and control groups, respectively, from study to study. Describe interesting, worthwhile studies that are not possible to include in a quantitative review.

(12) Describe the limitations of your review and provide guidelines for future research concerning the relationship reviewed.

(13) Remember Green and Hall's (1984: 52) dictum: "Data analysis is an aid to thought, not a substitute."

# REFERENCES

NOTE: Articles with an asterisk indicate applications of meta-analysis in contrast to methodologically focused articles (without asterisks).


ADCOCK, C. J. (1960) "A note on combining probabilities." Psychometrika 25: 303-305.
*ANDREWS, G., B. GUITAR, and P. HOWIE (1980) "Meta-analysis of the effects of stuttering treatment." Journal of Speech & Hearing Disorders 45: 287-307.
*BAKER, S. and C. POPOWICZ (1983) "Meta-analysis as a strategy for evaluating effects of career education interventions." Vocational Guidance Quarterly 3: 178-186.
*BASSOFF, E. and G. GLASS (1982) "The relationship between sex roles and mental health: A meta-analysis of twenty-six studies." Counseling Psychologist 10: 105-112.
BECKER, B. J. and L. V. HEDGES (1984) "Meta-analysis of cognitive gender differences: A comment on an analysis by Rosenthal and Rubin." Journal of Educational Psychology 76: 583-587.
BIRNBAUM, A. (1954) "Combining independent tests of significance." Journal of the American Statistical Association 49: 554-574.
*BOND, C. and L. TITUS (1983) "Social facilitation: A meta-analysis of 241 studies." Psychological Bulletin 94: 265-292.
CARLBERG, C. G., D. W. JOHNSON, R. JOHNSON, G. MARUYAMA, K. KAVALE, C-L. C. KULIK, J. A. KULIK, R. S. LYSAKOWSKI, S. W. PFLAUM, and H. J. WALBERG (1984) "Meta-analysis in education: A reply to Slavin." Educational Researcher 13(8): 16-23.
COCHRAN, W. G. (1937) "Problems arising in the analysis of a series of similar experiments." Journal of the Royal Statistical Society, Supplement 4: 102-118.
COHEN, J. (1977) Statistical Power Analysis for the Behavioral Sciences (revised ed.). New York: Academic Press.
———(1965) "Some statistical issues in psychology research," in B. Wolman (ed.) Handbook of Clinical Psychology. New York: McGraw-Hill.
*COHEN, P. (1980) "Effectiveness of student-rating feedback for improving college instruction: A meta-analysis of findings." Research in Higher Education 13: 321-341.
*———J. KULIK, and C-L. KULIK (1982) "Educational outcomes of tutoring: A meta-analysis of findings." American Educational Research Journal 19(2): 237-248.
COOK, T., and LEVITON, L. (1980) "Reviewing the literature: A comparison of traditional methods with meta-analysis." Journal of Personality 48: 449-472.
COOPER, H. M. (1984) The Integrative Research Review: A Systematic Approach. Beverly Hills, CA: Sage.
———(1982) "Scientific guidelines for conducting integrative research reviews." Review of Educational Research 52: 291-302.

58

*———(1979) "Statistically combining independent studies: A meta-analysis of sex differences in conformity research." Journal of Personality and Social Psychology 37: 131-146.

———and R. ARKIN (1981) "On quantitative reviewing." Journal of Personality 49: 225-230.

*COOPER, H., J. BURGER, and T. GOOD (1981) "Gender differences in the academic locus of control beliefs of young children." Journal of Personality and Social Psychology 40: 562-572.

COOPER, H. and R. ROSENTHAL (1980) "Statistical versus traditional procedures for summarizing research findings." Psychological Bulletin 87: 442-449.

*DEVINE, E. and T. COOK (1983) "A meta-analytic analysis of effects of psycho-educational interventions on length of postsurgical hospital stay." Nursing Research 32: 267-274.

*DUSEK, J. and G. JOSEPH (1983) "The bases of teacher expectancies: A meta-analysis." Journal of Educational Psychology 75: 327-346.

*DUSH, D., M. HIRT, and H. SCHROEDER (1983) "Self-statement modification with adults: A meta-analysis." Psychological Bulletin 94: 408-422.

EYSENCK, H. J. (1978) "An exercise in mega-silliness." American Psychologist 33: 517.

FEDERIGHI, E. T. (1959) "Extended tables of the percentage points of Student's t-distribution." Journal of the American Statistical Association 54: 683-688.

*FINDLEY, M. and H. COOPER (1983) "Locus of control and academic achievement: A literature review." Journal of Personality and Social Psychology 44: 419-427.

FISHER, R. A. (1948) "Combining independent tests of significance." American Statistician 2(5): 30.

———(1932) Statistical Methods for Research Workers (4th ed.). London: Oliver and Boyd.

FRIEDMAN, H. (1968) "Magnitude of experimental effect and a table for its rapid estimation." Psychological Bulletin 70: 245-251.

GALLO, P. S. (1978) "Meta-analysis: A mixed meta-phor." American Psychologist 33: 517.

*GETSIE, R. L., P. LANGER, and G. V. GLASS (1985) "Meta-analysis of the effects of type and combination of feedback on children's discrimination learning." Review of Educational Research 55: 9-22.

*GIACONIA, R. M. and L. V. HEDGES (1982) "Identifying features of effective open education." Review of Educational Research 52: 579-602.

*GILBERT, J., B. McPEEK, and F. MOSTELLER (1977) "Statistics and ethics in surgery and anesthesia." Science 198: 684-689.

GLASS, G. (1983) "Synthesizing empirical research: Meta-analysis," in S. A. Ward and L. J. Reed (eds.) Knowledge Structure and Use: Implications for Synthesis and Interpretation. Philadelphia: Temple University Press.

———(1977) "Integrating findings: The meta-analysis of research." Review of Research in Education 5: 351-379.

———(1976) "Primary, secondary, and meta-analysis of research." Educational Researcher 5: 3-8.

———B. McGAW, and M. L. SMITH (1981) Meta-Analysis in Social Research. Beverly Hills, CA: Sage.

*GLASS, G. and M. SMITH (1979) "Meta-analysis of research on class size and achievement." Educational Evaluation and Policy Analysis 1: 2-16.

GREEN, B. and J. HALL (1984) "Quantitative methods for literature review." Annual Review of Psychology 35: 37-53.

*HAASE, R., D. WAECHTER, and G. SOLOMON (1982) "How significant is a significant difference? Average effect size of research in counseling." Journal of Counseling Psychology 29: 58-65.

*HARRIS, M. J. and R. ROSENTHAL (1985) "Mediation of interpersonal expectancy effects: 31 meta-analyses." Psychological Bulletin 97: 363-386.

HAUSER-CRAM, P. (1983) "Some cautions in synthesizing research studies." Educational Evaluation and Policy Analysis 5: 155-162.

*HEAROLD, S. (1979) "Meta-analysis of the effects of television on social behavior." Presented at the annual meeting of the American Educational Research Association, San Francisco, April.

HEDGES, L. (1983) "A random effects model for effect sizes." Psychological Bulletin 93: 388-395.

———(1982a) "Estimation of effect size from a series of independent experiments." Psychological Bulletin 92: 490-499.

———(1982b) "Fitting categorical models to effect sizes from a series of experiments." Journal of Educational Statistics 7: 119-137.

———(1982c) "Fitting continuous models to effect size data." Journal of Educational Statistics 7: 245-270.

———(1981) "Distribution theory for Glass's estimator of effect size and related estimators." Journal of Educational Statistics 6: 107-128.

———and I. OLKIN (1985) Statistical Methods for Meta-Analysis. Orlando, FL: Academic Press.

———(1984) "Nonparametric estimators of effect size in meta-analysis." Psychological Bulletin 96: 573-580.

———(1983a) "Clustering estimates of effect magnitude from independent studies." Psychological Bulletin 93: 563-573.

———(1983b) "Regression models in research synthesis." American Statistician 37: 137-140.

———(1982) "Analyses, reanalyses, and meta-analysis." Contemporary Education Review 1: 157-165.

———(1980) "Vote-counting methods in research synthesis." Psychological Bulletin 88: 359-369.

*———and W. STOCK (1983) "The effects of class size: An examination of rival hypotheses." American Educational Research Journal 20: 63-85.

HODGES, J. L., Jr. and E. L. LEHMAN (1962) "Rank methods for combination of independent experiments in analysis of variance." Annals of Mathematical Statistics 33: 482-497.

HSU, L. (1980) "Tests of differences in $p$ levels as tests of differences in effect sizes." Psychological Bulletin 88: 705-708.

HUNTER, J. E., F. L. SCHMIDT, and G. B. JACKSON (1982) Meta-Analysis: Cumulating Research Findings Across Studies. Beverly Hills, CA: Sage.

*HYDE, J. (1981) "How large are cognitive gender differences?" American Psychologist 36: 892-901.

*IAFFALDANO, M. T. and P. M. MUCHINSKY (1985) "Job satisfaction and job performance: A meta-analysis." Psychological Bulletin 97: 251-273.

*IDE, J., J. PARKERSON, G. HAERTEL, and H. WALBERG (1981) "Peer group influence on educational outcomes: A quantitative synthesis." Journal of Educational Psychology 73: 472-484.

JACKSON, G. (1980) "Methods for integrative reviews." Review of Educational Research 50: 438-460.

*JOHNSON, D. W., G. MARUYAMA, R. JOHNSON, D. NELSON, and L. SKON (1981) "Effects of cooperative, competitive, and individualistic goal structures on achievement: a meta-analysis." Psychological Bulletin 89: 47-62.

JONES, L. and D. FISKE (1953) "Models for testing the significance of combined results." Psychological Bulletin 50: 375-382.

KATZ, B. M., L. A. MARASCUILO, and M. McSWEENEY (1985) "Nonparametric alternatives for testing main effects hypotheses: A model for combining data across independent studies." Psychological Bulletin 98: 200-208.

KOZIOL, J. A. and M. D. PERLMAN (1978) "Combining independent chi-squared tests." Journal of the American Statistical Association 73: 753-763.

KRAEMER, H. C. (1984) "Nonparametric effect size estimation: A reply." Psychological Bulletin 96: 569-572.

———(1983) "Theory of estimation and testing of effect sizes: Use in meta-analysis." Journal of Educational Statistics 8: 93-101.

———and G. ANDREWS (1982) "A nonparametric technique for meta-analysis effect size calculation." Psychological Bulletin 91: 404-412.

KRAUTH, J. (1983) "Nonparametric effect size estimation: A comment on Kraemer and Andrews." Psychological Bulletin 94: 190-192.

*KULIK, C. L. and J. KULIK (1982) "Effects of ability grouping on secondary school students: A meta-analysis of evaluation findings." American Educational Research Journal 19: 415-428.

*———and B. SHWALB (1983) "College programs for high-risk and disadvantaged students: A meta-analysis of findings." Review of Educational Research 53: 397-414.

KULIK, J. (1983) "Book review." Review of G. V. Glass et al., Meta-analysis in Social Research (Sage, 1981). Evaluation News 4: 101-105.

———C-L. C. KULIK, and P. A. COHEN (1979) "Meta-analysis of outcomes of Keller's Personalized System of Instruction." American Psychologist 34: 307-318.

*———(1980) "Effectiveness of computer-based college teaching: A meta-analysis of findings." Review of Educational Research 50: 525-544.

KUROSAWA, K. (1984) "Meta-analysis and selective publication bias." American Psychologist 39: 73-75.

*LANDMAN, J. and R. DAWES (1982) "Psychotherapy outcome: Smith and Glass' conclusions stand up under scrutiny." American Psychologist 37: 504-516.

LEVITON, L. and T. COOK (1981) "What differentiates meta-analysis from other forms of review?" Journal of Personality 49: 231-236.

LIGHT, R. J. [ed.] (1983) Evaluation Studies, Review Annual, Vol. 8. Beverly Hills, CA: Sage.

———and D. B. PILLEMER (1984) Summing Up: The Science of Reviewing Research. Cambridge, MA: Harvard University Press.

———(1982) "Numbers and narrative: Combining their strengths in research reviews." Harvard Educational Review 52: 1-26.

LIGHT, R. and P. SMITH (1971) "Accumulating evidence: Procedures for resolving contradictions among different research studies." Harvard Educational Review 41: 429-471.

*LINN, R. L. and C. N. HASTINGS (1984) "A meta-analysis of the validity of predictors of performance in law school." Journal of Educational Measurement 21: 245-259.
LITTELL, R. C. and J. L. FOLKS (1973) "Asymptotic optimality of Fisher's method of combining independent tests II," Journal of the American Statistical Association 68: 193-194.
———(1971) "Asymptotic optimality of Fisher's method of combining independent tests." Journal of the American Statistical Association 66: 802-806.
*LUITEN, J., W. AMES, and G. ACKERSON (1980) "A meta-analysis of the effects of advance organizers on learning and retention." American Educational Research Journal 17: 211-218.
*LYSAKOWSKI, R. and H. WALBERG (1982) "Instructional effects of cues, participation, and corrective feedback: A quantitative synthesis." American Educational Research Journal 19: 559-578.
*MABE, P. A. and S. G. WEST (1982) "Validity of self-evaluation of ability: A review and meta-analysis." Journal of Applied Psychology 67: 280-296.
MANSFIELD, R. S. and T. V. BUSSE (1977) "Meta-analysis of research: A rejoinder to Glass." Educational Researcher 6(10): 3.
*MAZZUCA, S. (1982) "Does patient education in chronic disease have therapeutic value?" Journal of Chronic Diseases 35: 521-529.
McGAW, B. and G. GLASS (1980) "Choice of the metric for effect size in meta-analysis." American Educational Research Journal 17: 325-337.
McGUIRE, J., G. W. BATES, B. J. DRETZKE, E. McGIVERN, K. L. REMBOLD, D. R. SEABOLD, B. M. TURPIN, and J. R. LEVIN (1985) "Methodological quality as a component of meta-analysis." Educational Psychologist 20: 1-5.
*MILLER, R. and J. BERMAN (1983) "The efficacy of cognitive behavior therapies: A quantitative review of the research evidence." Psychological Bulletin 94: 39-53.
MOSTELLER, F. M. and R. R. BUSH (1954) "Selected quantitative techniques," in G. Lindzey (ed.) Handbook of Social Psychology, Vol. 1. Cambridge, MA: Addison-Wesley.
*MUMFORD, E., H. J. SCHLESINGER, and G. GLASS (1982) "The effects of psychological intervention on recovery from surgery and heart attacks: An analysis of the literature." American Journal of Public Health 72: 141-151.
OLIVER, L. and A. SPOKANE (1983) "Research integration: Approaches, problems, and recommendations for research reporting." Journal of Counseling Psychology 30: 252-257.
ORWIN, R. G. (1983) "A fail-safe N for effect size." Journal of Educational Statistics 8: 157-159.
———and D. S. CORDRAY (1985) "Effects of deficient reporting on meta-analysis: A conceptual framework and reanalysis." Psychological Bulletin 97: 134-147.
———(1984) "Smith and Glass's psychotherapy conclusions need further probing: On Landman and Dawes' reanalysis." American Psychologist 39: 71-73.
OZER, D. J. (1985) "Correlation and the coefficient of determination." Psychological Bulletin 97: 307-315.
PEARSON, K. (1933) "On a method of determining whether a sample of size n supposed to have been drawn from a parent population having a known probability integral has probably been drawn at random." Biometrika 25: 379-410.
*PETERS, L. H., D. D. HARTKE, and J. T. POHLMANN (1985) "Fiedler's contingency theory of leadership: An application of the meta-analysis procedures of Schmidt and Hunter." Psychological Bulletin 97: 274-285.

PILLEMER, D. and R. LIGHT (1980) "Synthesizing outcomes: How to use research evidence from many studies." Harvard Educational Review 50: 176-195.

*POSAVAC, E. (1980) "Evaluation of patient education programs." Evaluation and the Health Professions 3: 47-62.

*———J. M. SINACORE, S. E. BROTHERTON, M. C. HELFORD, and R. S. TURPIN (1985) "Increasing compliance to medical treatment regimens." Evaluation and the Health Professions 8: 7-22.

PRESBY, S. (1978) "Overly broad categories obscure important differences between therapies." American Psychologist 33: 514-515.

RIMLAND, B. (1979) "Death knell for psychotherapy?" American Psychologist 34: 192.

ROSENTHAL, R. (1984) Meta-Analytic Procedures for Social Research. Beverly Hills, CA: Sage.

———(1983) "Assessing the statistical and social importance of the effects of psychotherapy." Journal of Consulting and Clinical Psychology 51: 4-13.

———(1980a) "On telling tails when combining results of independent studies." Psychological Bulletin 88: 496-497.

———[ed.] (1980b) Quantitative Assessment of Research Domains. San Francisco: Jossey-Bass.

———(1979) "The 'file drawer' problem and tolerance for null results." Psychological Bulletin 86: 638-641.

———(1978a) "Combining results of independent studies." Psychological Bulletin 65: 185-193.

*———(1978b) "Interpersonal expectancy effects: The first 345 studies." Behavioral and Brain Sciences 3: 377-415.

———and R. L. ROSNOW (1984) Essentials of Behavioral Research. New York: McGraw-Hill.

ROSENTHAL, R. and D. RUBIN (1983) "Ensemble-adjusted p values." Psychological Bulletin 94: 540-541.

———(1982a) "A simple, general purpose display of magnitude of experimental effect." Journal of Educational Psychology 74: 166-169.

———(1982b) "Comparing effect sizes of independent studies." Psychological Bulletin 92: 500-504.

———(1982c) "Further meta-analytic procedures for assessing cognitive gender differences." Journal of Educational Psychology 74: 708-712.

———(1979) "Comparing significance levels of independent studies." Psychological Bulletin 86: 1165-1168.

ROSSI, P. and S. WRIGHT (1977) "Evaluation research: An assessment of theory, practice, and politics." Evaluation Quarterly 1: 5-52.

*ROTTON, J. and I. W. KELLY (1985) "Much ado about the full moon: A meta-analysis of lunar-lunacy research." Psychological Bulletin 97: 286-306.

*SCHMIDT, F. L., I. GAST-ROSENBERG, and J. E. HUNTER (1980) "Validity generalization: Results for computer programmers." Journal of Applied Psychology 65: 643-661.

SECHREST, L. and W. H. YEATON (1982) "Magnitudes of experimental effects in social science research." Evaluation Review 6: 579-600.

*SHAPIRO, D. and D. SHAPIRO (1982) "Meta-analysis of comparative therapy outcome studies: A replication and refinement." Psychological Bulletin 92: 581-604.

SLAVIN, R. (1984) "Meta-analysis in education: How has it been used?" Educational Researcher 3(18): 6-15.

————(1983) "Meta-nonsense: Misuse of meta-analysis in educational research." Presented at the annual meeting of the American Educational Research Association, Montreal.

*SMITH, M. and G. GLASS (1980) "Meta-analysis of research on class size and its relationship to attitudes and instruction." American Educational Research Journal 17: 419-433.

*————(1977) "Meta-analysis of psychotherapy outcome studies." American Psychologist 32: 752-760.

*STEINKAMP, M. and M. MAEHR (1983) "Affect, ability, and science achievement: A quantitative synthesis of correlational research." Review of Educational Research 53: 369-396.

STOCK, W., M. OKUM, M. HARING, W. MILLER, C. KINNEY, and R. CEURVORST (1982) "Rigor in data synthesis: A case study of reliability in meta-analysis." Educational Researcher 11(6): 10-20.

STOUFFER, S. A., E. A. SUCHMAN, L. C. De VINNEY, S. A. STAR, and R. M. WILLIAMS, Jr. (1949) The American Soldier: Adjustment During Army Life, Vol. 1. Princeton, NJ: Princeton University Press.

STRUBE, M. J. (1985) "Combining and comparing significance levels from nonindependent hypothesis tests." Psychological Bulletin 97: 334-341.

————and D. HARTMANN (1982a) "Meta-analysis: Techniques, applications, and functions." Journal of Consulting and Clinical Psychology 51: 14-27.

————(1982b) "A critical appraisal of meta-analysis." British Journal of Clinical Psychology 21: 129-139.

H. K. SUEN (1984) "A Bayesian aggregate meta-analytic evaluation approach." Evaluation and the Health Professions 7: 461-470.

TALLMADGE, G. K. (1977) The Joint Dissemination Review Panel Ideabook. Washington, DC: National Institute of Education and U.S. Office of Education.

TIPPETT, L.H.C. (1931) The Methods of Statistics. London: Williams and Norgate.

TRACZ, S. M., I. NEWMAN, and K. McNEIL (1985) "Regression techniques and dependence of data in meta-analysis." Presented at the annual meetings of the Mid-Western Educational Research Association, Chicago.

TUKEY, J. W. (1977) Exploratory Data Analysis. Reading, MA: Addison-Wesley.

van ZWET, W. R. and J. OSTERHOFF (1967) "On the combination of independent test statistics." Annals of Mathematical Statistics 38: 659-680.

VIANA, M. (1980) "Statistical methods for summarizing independent correlational results." Journal of Educational Statistics 5: 83-104.

WARD, S. A. and L. J. REED [eds.] (1983) Knowledge Structure and Use: Implications for Synthesis and Interpretation. Philadelphia: Temple University Press.

*WELCH, W. W. and H. J. WALBERG (1970) "Pretest and sensitization effects in curriculum evaluation." American Educational Research Journal 7: 605-614.

*WHITE, K. (1982) "The relation between socioeconomic status and academic achievement." Psychological Bulletin 91: 461-481.

*WHITLEY, B. (1983) "Sex role orientation and self-esteem: A critical meta-analytic review." Journal of Personality and Social Psychology 44: 765-778.

*WILLIAMS, P., E. HAERTEL, G. HAERTEL, and H. WALBERG (1982) "The impact of leisure-time television on school learning: A research synthesis." American Educational Research Journal 19: 19-50.

*WILLSON, V. and R. PUTNAM (1982) "A meta-analysis of pretest sensitization effects in experimental design." American Educational Research Journal 19: 249-258.

WINER, B. J. (1971) Statistical Principals in Experimental Design (2nd ed.). New York: McGraw-Hill.

WOLF, F. M. (1982) "Meta-analytic applications in program evaluation." Presented at the annual meeting of the American Psychological Association, Washington, DC. (ERIC Document Reproduction Service No. ED 225 049)

*———and S. L. BLIXT (1981) "A cross-sectional cross-lagged panel analysis of mathematics achievement and attitudes: Implications for the interpretation of the direction of predictive validity." Educational and Psychological Measurement 41: 829-834.

WOLF, F. M. and R. G. CORNELL (forthcoming) "Interpreting behavioral, biomedical, and psychological correlations in chronic disease using $2 \times 2$ tables." Journal of Chronic Disease 39.

*WOLF, F. M., M. L. SAVICKAS, G. A. SALTZMAN, and M. L. WALKER (1984) "Meta-analytic evaluation of an interpersonal skills curriculum for medical students: Synthesizing evidence over successive occasions." Journal of Counseling Psychology 31: 253-257.

WOLF, F. M. and C. J. SPIES (1981) "Assessing the consistency of cross-lagged panel effects with the Fisher Combined Test." Proceedings of the American Statistical Association Social Statistics Section 24: 506-511.

WORTMAN, P. (1983) "Evaluation research: A methodological perspective." Annual Review of Psychology 34: 223-260.

*———and W. YEATON (1983) "Synthesis of results in controlled trials of coronary artery bypass graft surgery," in R. J. Light (ed.) Evaluation Studies Review Annual, Vol. 8. Beverly Hills, CA: Sage.

YEATON, W. H., and P. M. WORTMAN [eds.] (1984) Issues in Data Synthesis. New Directions for Program Evaluation, No. 24. San Francisco: Jossey-Bass.

YIN, R. K., E. BINGHAM, and K. A. HEALD (1976) "The difference that quality makes: The case of literature reviews." Sociological Methods and Research 5: 139-156.

FREDRIC M. WOLF *is Assistant Professor of Postgraduate Medicine and Health Professions Education and Co-Director of Educational Development and Evaluation of the Diabetes Research and Training Center at the University of Michigan. He holds a B.A. in political science from the University of Wisconsin, an M.A. in learning and development, and a Ph.D. in educational psychology and in evaluation and measurement from Kent State University. He has published numerous articles on evaluation, problem solving, decision making, and social-psychological aspects of chronic illness which have appeared in scholarly journals, including the* Journal of the American Medical Association, Journal of Counseling Psychology, Journal of Educational Psychology, Evaluation and the Health Professions, *and* Journal of Consulting and Clinical Psychology.